JOHNNYSWIM

JOHNNYSWIM
HOME SWEET ROAD

FINDING LOVE, MAKING MUSIC, AND BUILDING A LIFE ONE CITY AT A TIME

Convergent / New York

This is a work of nonfiction. Some names and identifying details have been changed.

Copyright © 2021 by Mr. and Mrs. Swim, LLC
Foreword by Chip and Joanna Gaines copyright © 2021 by Penguin Random House LLC

Published in the United States by Convergent Books, an imprint of Random House,
a division of Penguin Random House LLC, New York.

CONVERGENT BOOKS is a registered trademark and its C colophon is a trademark of
Penguin Random House LLC.

Photograph credits are located on page 255.

LIBRARY OF CONGRESS CATALOGING-IN-PUBLICATION DATA
Names: Johnnyswim (Musical group), author.
Title: Home sweet road / Johnnyswim.
Description: First edition. | New York: Convergent, 2021. |
Identifiers: LCCN 2021004343 (print) | LCCN 2021004344 (ebook) |
ISBN 9780593160206 (hardcover) | ISBN 9780593160213 (ebook)
Subjects: LCSH: Johnnyswim (Musical group) | Singers—United States—
Biography. | LCGFT: Biographies.
Classification: LCC ML421.J636 J66 2021 (print) | LCC ML421.J636
(ebook) | DDC 782.42164092/2 [B]—dc23
LC record available at https://lccn.loc.gov/2021004343
LC ebook record available at https://lccn.loc.gov/2021004344

Printed in the United States of America on acid-free paper

crownpublishing.com

2 4 6 8 9 7 5 3 1

First Edition

Design: Smith & Shulman / designSimple
Creative Direction: Mike McGlaflin

For our parents,
without whom we'd have no sail.
And for our children,
without whom we'd have no anchor.

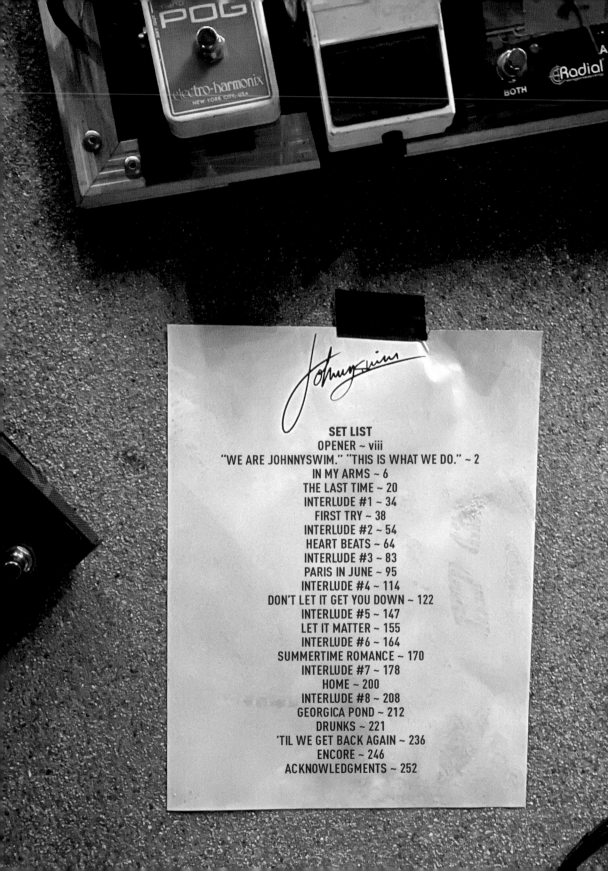

Johnnyswim (signature)

SET LIST

BEFORE WE EVER LEARNED ANYTHING ABOUT ABNER AND Amanda, we knew JOHNNYSWIM. Listening to "Diamonds" for the first time, we were captivated by the way it encompassed the fullness of life—in all its beauty and all its brokenness. Yet that's how it is with all their songs: The lyrics tell familiar stories that feel as though they could be our own. We had an immediate connection to JOHNNYSWIM's music—so much so that we asked them to play at Chip's fortieth birth-day party, which is when we realized that these two were the real deal. Soon after that, we asked if we could use their song "Home" for the opener of *Fixer Upper*. It's now many years later, and that song has be-come a sort of anthem of ours. Since then, we've welcomed their band onto the stage to play at our annual Silobration five times in a row.

Over those years, we've moved beyond being starstruck by JOHNNYSWIM and have found a deep friendship with Abner and Amanda.

They are the kind of folks you want to sit around the fire with way too late into the night, just lost in conversation. Everything about them is dynamic and compelling. How could it not be? Theirs is a life of dichotomy: the daughter of a celebrity and the son of immigrants; in the spotlight as rock stars and changing diapers as parents; living fast-paced, crazy days on the road and slow, simple days at home; epitomizing both the dreamy power couple and the most down-to-earth people in the world.

There's a certain kind of magic that follows Amanda and Abner wherever they go. A sort of warmth that draws you back to them, and, once you feel it, you can't help but notice that it's in everything they do. It's in their music and lyrics, in how they're somehow always able to use words that go straight to the heart. It's around their dinner table, in the food they prepare and the stories they tell. It's in their community, in the way this group of mismatched people have become family. It's in the way they parent, in the way their kids are growing up to be curious and kind. It's simply in the way they look at life, and in how, even in the hard times, they somehow go about

their days with ease and grace. And it's in the pages of this book, in the raw stories and candid photographs.

We felt their magic the moment we first met them at Chip's birthday party and have been lucky enough to have a front-row seat to it ever since. And we're excited for you to feel it, too, and to be inspired by the life that Amanda and Abner have created together. They are a gift to this world—not only in song, but in who they are as people.

—Chip and Joanna Gaines

FOREWORD

JOHNNYSWIM
HOME SWEET ROAD

"WE ARE JOHNNYSWIM."

IF HOME IS WHERE THE HEART IS, then we've been making home all over these forty-eight contiguous states and beyond since 2005. Highway by highway, state by state, stage by stage, we've nurtured our love and our family. Then we set out the welcome mat. Everyone's invited. Each venue is our living room, and each show is a party we're throwing for our closest friends. It just so happens most of them are strangers.

And now, fifteen or so years in, we've been tasked with giving you a glimpse into our little whirlwind of a life, walking you through the sights, sounds, laughter, joy, and tastes of a life built—and growing—on the road. To be honest, it's an intimidating task. We've never done anything like this before, but Hemingway said (At least I *think* he said it. Let's just say he did.) writing is easy: "All you have to do is sit at the typewriter and bleed." So here we go. Only, bleeding is a little too messy and we already have three kids to clean up after, so instead, we hope to invite you into our veins, into the currents of what drives us and the life force it carries.

A family member once described our life and schedule as her "absolute nightmare." How sweet. We are self-employed, married to our business/creative partner, working on the road, and raising a family on highways and in dressing rooms. We

get it. It sounds a little wild. And, thankfully, it is. The chaos is as cozy to us as a blanket at this point.

Constantly being on your toes teaches you a few things along the way. Like how much community matters and the importance of probiotics while traveling. One thing we do know for absolute certain is that chasing down something you feel called to do will cost you. We have certainly felt those costs. Sometimes it requires more energy than you have. Other times it requires more patience or tenacity, but most of all, it requires you to be a constant professional at silencing the voice that says, *You're an idiot for thinking you are qualified for any of this in the first place!* In many ways, that's the hardest part, silencing the voice. But it's important work, allowing us to continue to live out this calling we are so grateful for. Our journey, much like yours, is bespoke to us, tailor-made. It's all we've ever wanted. But even if, like our previously mentioned family member, you think it sounds horrible, we still hope you'll take a little of our passion with you.

The thing is, we don't have to sell out another show to feel like we've "made it." We've got no trophy case or extraordinary accolades, we've never even been nominated for anything, and we still have dozens of dreams ahead of us yet to be

3

realized. But for us, we *have* made it. We get to pour out our hearts and show our babies: "You can have your cake and eat it, too. You can do what you love with the people you love."

Sometimes we wrestle with feeling like we might not be capable of living the life we've always wanted. It can be very hard to take your home on the road. "I believe; help my unbelief" should be the life mantra of two traveling troubadours with three babies. Like a high-wire act performed with nothing to catch us if we fall, we often talk about what it means to live life "without a net." That's us!

In the middle of this beautiful circus, we have made a home. Raising babies and chasing dreams with no net to catch us is the only life we've ever wanted. These are the good old days. You're invited. Come on in. The water is fine . . . ish . . . sometimes. It's all good. We're gonna have a blast. *That* we know for sure. Here goes nothing!

"THIS IS WHAT WE DO."

Amanda

It doesn't matter where we are
Stuck in the rain in Central Park
Driving down Sunset Boulevard
If you're there in my arms.

IN MY ARMS

WAKING UP IS HARD FOR ME. I'M a natural sleeper. I'm neither a morning person nor a night owl. I'm one of those people who thrives only between 10:00 A.M. and 4:00 P.M. Outside of that, I'm just okay. I can't promise I'm going to be my best self. This morning is no different, except there's a slightly red hue to the morning rays sneaking through the curtain, so I'm more confused than normal. We live in Burbank, California, where I know the light so well, I can tell the time based on the shadows cast across our bedroom. This morning is different, though.

I hear our sweet new baby, Paloma, chirping in her crib, making the sweetest little sounds on earth. I pick her up and give her breakfast, also known in our family as a "booby snack," while enjoying some delicious baby cuddles in my half-comatose state. Abner must have snuck out while I was still snoozing, which is good news for me, because that means there's probably coffee ready.

I whine, "Oh my gooooodness" into the baby monitor (our little cue since our first year of marriage that I'm awake and, for that reason, slightly unhappy), and within two minutes he's at the door with some wake-up juice.

Thank you, Jesus, for such a thoughtful husband.

When we first got married, Abner noticed that whole not-being-a-morning-person thing about me. And ever since, he won't let me get out of bed unless he brings me coffee first. If you want to know how to make a happy marriage, that's how, my friends.

I hand Paloma over to Abner and start my daily search for clean clothes. Laundry is hard to do sometimes, and even when it's done, it rarely gets put away. We just sort of dig out what we need until it's all back to being dirty. What is a dresser again? I can't remember. Oh well. I'll just wear the same sweats I've been wearing for two days, the same hoodie, the same

shoes. It's all right there, shoved into a little closet behind our bed. Clean underwear is really all you need. And, lucky me, though I'm down to my last pair, at least I'm good for the day. Who cares about fashion or style? Just don't ask the twenty-year-old me that question. *What does she know? She was inexperienced at life and over-rested.*

I'm dressed and walking up the dark hallway. It seems everyone is awake and up front or already gone. Sure enough, when I get through the door to the open kitchen/living area, my bigger babies are jumping around, spilling cereal, and squealing at the sight of me. Luna, our second, is in full toddler mode, trying to climb out of her highchair, which is screwed to the table. She is screaming, per usual. Is it a happy scream, a sad scream, an angry scream, a scared scream? Who can know? Toddlers are a mystery Heaven has given us to stretch our capacities and the limits of our sanity, all wrapped up in the cutest possible package so we don't throw ourselves directly in the garbage. Luna is no different. She is simultaneously all the work and all the delight.

I pick her up, wipe her off, and snack on her cheeks for a minute. Joaquin, her big brother and our oldest, immediately* begs to come with us to work today. Of course, the answer is yes. But Amy, our nanny, has now walked in. She tells him about a cool museum nearby, and he no longer cares about old Mom and Dad. He's got plans now. He runs back to find some clothes out of said clean-clothes pile. He is joy in human form. Unfortunately, getting him dressed looks like a Cirque du Soleil show and takes about as long. It requires stretching and two minutes of meditation before beginning. Finally, he's ready. He heads down the stairs with Luna and Amy, and hops on the kickstand of our enormous mini-van of a stroller. I miss them already, but I've got to go.

I fumble around, looking for the shoes I took off last night. Finally, I find them and throw them into my bag along with my security badge, which I'm shocked I haven't already lost. I swing the door open and step out. I'm in a parking garage. No wonder it's so dark this morning. I look down for a green arrow, and

---

* What I mean by "immediately" is that Joaquin begs us for this after twenty pleas for screen time that have all been met with nos. He's got plenty of unique and awesome things he can get into right outside the door, and we want him to spend his energy eating up the world around him, not always getting sucked into worlds made in Hollywood or, worse, Burbank. Plus, we want to use screen time for when we need him to be quiet or chill. It's our secret weapon and not to be overused, otherwise it loses its power. Clearly, we are professional parents.

sure enough, it's right next to the door mat, thanks to our tour manager, Greg. It's pointing me to the right. I step out. And as I turn, I remember . . . I'm in Colorado.[†] This is the legendary Red Rocks Amphitheater. We're playing here for the first time, tonight.

I lock the tour bus behind me. This is going to be a great day.

It doesn't matter where we go
East Tennessee or Tokyo
I'm not a foreigner, I'm home
When you're there in my arms.

† As I said earlier, we live in Burbank and we love it, but we don't want people to know how cool it is because then all the dumdums will move there and make it horrible.

So here we go. Book-writing time. *[Cracks knuckles, stretches neck, takes sip of water . . . walks away from keyboard . . . for a few days.]*

All right, we're back. First of all, I want to make it clear that I mean every word of what I'm about to say.

Church is a great place to meet chicks. Maybe even the best place.

[Presses Print. Collects Pulitzer.]

Abner

I WAS NINETEEN YEARS OLD WHEN Amanda changed my life. Nineteen! It seems literally impossible for that age to be as far in the past as it feels now. Wow. I was a child. The only reason I had attended church in Brentwood, Tennessee, that day was that I was dating a girl who was no longer okay with our philandering unless I agreed to go to a service with her.

Now, don't get me wrong. I was no longtime listener/first-time caller. I grew up in church. Three days a week, *minimum.* Twice on Sundays. Anyone else who grew up in the Southern Baptist church in the Deep South knows what I'm talking about. The sweet guilt that dripped from those speakers drew us like moths to a flame. "Please, tell me more about how worthless I am!" Riveting stuff. But I *loved* it. I loved being at church, loved my friends, loved the community that it created (even if we were only there to get yelled at). Most of all, I loved the music.

The church I grew up in was the kind that had over a hundred people in the choir and a full orchestra with a string section and everything. They definitely knew how to play the long game. Sometime around when I was seven years old, the church began to offer free lessons and instrument rentals to anyone willing to play in the church orchestra who didn't quite yet have the skill set to join. I started lessons at that young age, and by the time I was thirteen I was in both the orchestra and the youth band.

When I was a teenager, my Sundays consisted of morning youth worship and Sunday school, followed by the "big church" service (worship and a message again, but with grownups), then a Sunday-night service, followed most weeks by a youth event. There was Monday-night visitation, where we'd proselytize door to door, asking folks that legendary question: "Do you know that you know that you know where you'd spend eternity, if you died today?" Tuesday-night youth band practice. Wednesday-night service, followed by a full orchestra rehearsal. Saturdays, I'd normally end up in the youth building trying to figure out how to play guitar and work the sound equipment. (There is an astonishing amount of bad recordings we made in that room trying to figure out how to work the gear and how to write songs at the same time.) Then, on Sunday, we'd start all over.

This about sums up my childhood and teenage years. Not a whole lot of philandering (or as we knew it then, "backsliding") was happening in those years. We had all basically joined a special club we were certain had all the answers to life's biggest questions.

• • •

So now I'm nineteen years old, living alone in Nashville, Tennessee. I'm no longer at church 326 times a week for years on end. And to be honest, I'm not real sure about all that fire-and-brimstone stuff. This is like my one year of being a mess and stirring up trouble. I meet a girl, and she tells me I have to come to church with her in order for our "thing" to keep going. So, yeah, I know the church game. . . . I'm fine playing it.

Then, there in that Nashville church with my girlfriend, after years and years of attending church, I finally see my first miracle. Church has just wrapped, and the pastor dismisses the congregation. The Miracle is the first to stand, and the rest of the room sits in silent awe and rapt attention to honor the rising of this angelic visitor (maybe I'm just imagining all of this?). White sweater, blue jeans, curly hair, perfect cheekbones, poise, confidence . . . just plain *gorgeous*. I'm most certainly not imagining *this*.

That's the girl I'm going to marry. I'm sitting there next to the girl I'm dating, not just *thinking* these words. I also— very much out loud, with my mouth— say, "That's the girl I'm going to marry!"

All at once, everything goes from moving in slow motion to full speed as I'm jarred by a swift elbow to the ribs. My girlfriend is *pissed*. "I guess you better go talk to her, then," she snaps.

I'm still so shaken by that glimpse of The Miracle that I don't even register Girlfriend's indignation. My only answer is a dull "Yeah . . . I think you're right." I get up out of my seat with no real plan—I just know that I absolutely need to meet this girl. I have no idea who she is, but I know that whatever force squeezed those words from my head down to my lungs and out of my mouth is the same force now propelling my legs.

I can't even imagine what I look like as I make my way upstream, heading to the front of the room, while everyone heads out the back. Maybe I'm being rude as I rush through these fellow well-intentioned parishioners, but I'm also determined to have something stunning to say as an offering to this goddess. A plan quickly forms. I devise three

exiting-church strategies that make for good "meet cutes":

1) The Oopsie Daisy: This plan relies on the art of achieving physical interaction while creating the illusion that it is accidental. It basically involves walking into the object of your attraction, then saying, "Oopsie daisy!" First, you watch her, to plan the optimal moment of attack by looking not directly but just beyond or around her. Then, when she is least likely to be watching the path in front of her, you look in the direction that is farthest away from her (no more than a 90-degree turn of the neck) while squaring your shoulders directly toward her and taking a few confident steps right into her path. If done correctly, this encounter will seem completely accidental; it helps if there are a few of your acquaintances in her vicinity whom you can pretend to be approaching, to garner plausibility for this "accident."

2) The Gotcha: Though this plan does not engage her in a physical interaction like the Oopsie Daisy, in my opinion, this tactic is even bolder. Basically, you try to make it look like you've caught her looking at you. You watch her until you can predict that her gaze is going to cross your general vicinity, then you look away and quickly look back, acting like you've caught her looking at you.

Okay—this plan is terrible.

I decide to not even consider plan number 3, which is a variation on the Gotcha called I'm Going to Stare at You Until You Look at Me.

As it turns out, I use *none* of these plans. Halfway into plan number 1 (in review, that's the one where I walk into her and act like it was an accident so I can start a conversation), we actually end up genuinely making eye contact by accident. I have every line a church player like me can dream up, ready and waiting in my quiver. But in the time it takes me to start with "Oopsie daisy" or "Look at God," she looks at me . . . then actually rolls her eyes.

I never get to say a word.
I am crushed.
Ruined.
I sit down in the nearest seat and end up being the last one out of the building. When I get into my car alone and girl-friendless, I realize I need to work on me a little. Or a lot.

I'm basically prowling church like it's a nightclub, for goodness' sake.

This is an invitation to do some soul-searching, to say the least.

· · ·

The moment that wasn't was one that changed me for good. I never had another breakup, for one thing. I couldn't settle for anything less than the girl I saw at church that day.

The last time I saw someone I wanted was the first time I saw you.

But really, as the next four years passed, I learned a very deep and nuanced lesson: Stop being a douchebag. I never

dated again until I met my last girlfriend four years later over coffee. I finally found out The Miracle was named Amanda Grace Sudano.

The first thing I thought was that my last thought would be of you.

Amanda

THE STORY OF ABNER AND MY meeting spans about four years. It started one Sunday morning when I, an overachieving college student, decided to crawl out from my hobbit hole of books and papers and go to church. I'd been going to the same church for a while, but this one Sunday in particular I was sitting in the back and noticed a new and very cute guy standing up in the front to leave early. This took place on a couple of Sundays before Abner initially saw me. I remember the very first thought I had when I saw him: *That guy is so cute. He looks like he could be my brother.*

Typing those sentences now, I realize those are two phrases that should probably not go next to each other while describing a boy you're romantically interested in, but whatever. Who or what can control a young girl's weird postpubescent mind? It didn't matter anyway, because my second thought after that was one of certainty: *He'll never be into me.*

I knew this as soon as I saw the flock of beautiful girls surrounding Abner as he walked out. They weren't just any beautiful girls, either. These girls basically ran the church. I knew them, and I knew they didn't like me. It was a real-life *Mean Girls* situation. They were a popular and seemingly pious clique (their actual piety remains in question; no judgment—or maybe a little judgment) who came ready for the Lord's day with full hair, makeup, and fake lashes. I was the type who showed up having brushed her teeth, and maybe her hair, every other Sunday. I was and am a low-maintenance nerd, so if that was his crowd, I could go ahead and kill all those butterflies swimming in my guts. He, for sure, would never be into me. What a bummer. There was a cute guy right in my line of sight, and I would never ever even talk to him. That would forever be that. I would just have to resign myself to stalking him online when my Internet bandwidth wasn't overloaded from my downloading songs on Napster. (Yes, I'm old.)

The problem, unfortunately, for me was that this church and the city of Nashville, where the church met, were small worlds. And I kept seeing Abner around with mutual friends. I didn't like this. He was clearly trouble, and I was no dummy. I had watched a lot of chick flicks and knew what was up. He was the cute, flirtatious, popular guy who makes the lead girl fall in love only to crush her dreams and distract her from the guy who's the real love interest. We all know this. Tale as old as time.

So I did what any smart girl with limited confidence would do: I ignored him completely. Like on that fateful Sunday when he first saw me and tried to say hello. My go-to moves were to walk by him as if in a hurry or, if he moved in my direction, simply to turn my back abruptly, as if a fire had spontaneously erupted nearby. If, God forbid, we made eye contact by accident, which happened a time or two, I had no choice but to shove down all my hormonal responses and literally rush as fast as possible toward the nearest exit. I'm sure I looked super smooth.

Any of you who came here for lessons in love and romance, I gotchu. Clearly, you came to the right place.

• • •

One time, I drove up to the valet at the mall and realized the attendant was Abner, and on this particular day, he was the only one parking cars. An encounter was inevitable. I panicked and once again thought of all my options. I could get out and say, "Hi, I think we have some mutual friends. I'm Amanda. So nice to finally meet you. Here are my car keys." Of course, if I said that, he probably wouldn't remember me and would think I was flirting—and flirting poorly, at that.

That's a no.

My next option was to get out and just confidently toss him my keys without a word or glance, but then again, what if he did remember me? Then he would think I was horrible and rude.

That's no good, either.

I was stuck. So, since being a normal human wasn't an option, I chose to speed off to the back of the mall, park a mile away, and walk in through the back entrance for employees.

Pro move, Amanda. Pro. Move.

Soon after that day, I moved to New York to pursue music. I didn't see Abner again for about four years.

Fresh out of college, I had no real plan, which thrilled my parents, I'm sure. I had a dream of being a singer and songwriter, something they could relate to, but honestly I am not sure they had even heard me sing in my semi-adult life outside of school choir functions. I was, and still am, cripplingly shy in so many ways, and annoyingly overly self-aware. They would often ask me to sing for them and their friends when I was growing up, and I would always refuse.

"But, Amanda, how can you want to be a singer when you won't ever sing for people?" my mom would ask.

"Do you sing for people for free, Mom? I didn't think so. Pay up, and we'll see what I can do for you."

We'd have a good laugh. But, in reality, they were right, and my honest answer should have been a firm "I have no idea."

My dad's hope for me thrived despite the obvious character flaws keeping me from achieving my goals. He didn't seem to notice what I lacked, and if he did, he didn't let on. What I think my dad saw all those years my talent was still buried in the dirt waiting to sprout was a passion for music that came from him as much as my mother, if not more. He was the one to take me to the record store to use my allowance, quizzing me as we strolled the aisles on who wrote and produced what. He was the one for whom I would make mixtapes of songs I was listening to that I knew he'd love, too. He was the one who made it all real. My dad was less worried about my fear of performing and even my lack of skill. He knew the love of music itself would be enough fuel to get me where I needed to be, even and especially when I doubted myself.

I remember sitting in my little apartment, fresh to New York City, alone and wildly overwhelmed at the vision I had for myself—this calling I'd felt since I was a teenager. It towered over me like a mountain. I had no idea how to even start climbing it, let alone a clue as to how I would get to the top. It was a daunting and scary thought, and I felt like it required attributes I didn't naturally possess. I didn't have hustle or drive, and I didn't even feel particularly good at singing or songwriting. All I had was that sheer love for it. I remember wishing I could want to be something else: "Dear Jesus, can't I be passionate about accounting instead, or be a teacher or a nurse? Something that helps people and has a clear path to success. Not this floaty creative music thing."

This prayer was met with a resounding no from above. *Nice try,* God said, *but no ma'am.*

I am so often grateful for His nos. They're often more important than His yeses.

Amanda

WHAT WAS IT LIKE HAVING DONNA
Summer for a mother? So many people have asked me this that it rivals people saying, "How are you today?" or "What is your name?"

This question clued me in early on to our family's being a little different. Even when I was in elementary school, kids who still picked their noses openly would bring up my mother, clearly not because they knew or cared about who she was but because their parents had told them to ask. Pretty weird. Believe it or not, I never became close friends with any of those kids, and their parents probably never got the response they were hoping for.

I answer it now without even thinking. It has been on auto response since about 1984, the year I started forming sentences.

Generally, the conversation goes something like this:

"So, I have to ask, what was it like having Donna Summer as your mom?"

"Do you have a mom?" I reply. "It was sort of like that."

It sounds like a sassy answer, and you know what? It sort of *is*. But the older I've gotten, the less sassy that same answer has become. I used to say it, proud to have a quippy response, to defuse the antici-pation the question itself conjured. But lately, it's different. Lately, it's loaded and fragile. Now not having her, now being a mother myself, I realize how much of a mother my mother really was. My quippy little response has weight now.

The assumption, presumably, was that my family lived a life filled with private jets and celebrities lingering around the house, parents in black-tie dress while supper was served by a staff of twenty, large allowances, and nannies who cared for us while my parents paid attention to "more important things." If any of these things ever existed, I wasn't around for them. Of course, my mom and dad had help. They recorded and toured and had meetings, and my sisters and I were well supervised and cared for by others in those moments. But my greatest memories of my mother, the ones that feel the most real and have the most flesh on them eight years after she's left us, aren't of her on stages wowing crowds or levitating on the glorious applause of strangers. It's those memories of her tucking my little knobby legs in between hers to keep me warm all those nights I snuck into her bed, scared or restless or just wanting a cuddle. None of my children has tried coming into our room to sleep in the bed with me. Not even once. I am a selfish and angry sleeper. They can sense this; they've never even asked. She, somehow, regardless of her jet lag or fatigue, could mother even in her sleep.

And her voice—that timeless treasure—is seared into my brain. And not just in melodies. Those are epic. What I hear is her putting on a comedic, over-the-top cockney accent to purposefully wake my sisters and me up on Saturday mornings so we can have breakfast together. We loved to hate this habit she formed, and hated loving it. We'd beg her to stop, then come downstairs, unable to suppress our grins. This went on for years. She loved a long-standing joke. She knew it could bring people together and knot them there, even, and especially, when they struggled to escape.

She was aggravating in her caring for us the way only someone with an irrational level of love can be. She never let us leave the house with wet hair, and she was majorly annoying in making us wear extra layers because *she* was cold (not because *we* were cold; that was useless information—what mattered here was exclusively *her* temperature and her temperature only). She would yell at me for not making my bed even in college, and

she'd insist on me waking her up when I got home late so she knew I was safe. She wanted to know all my friends (and prank call them on occasion for fun), but she could barely help move me into my first dorm room because she was crying in the car and didn't want me to see her. She'd email me chain letters about random safety hazards regardless of their accuracy, just in case they might be right. She prayed over me every night and made sure I tasted every kind of food at least once. She was the most *mom* of any mom.

So if you're wondering what it was like growing up as the kid of Donna Summer, well, if you have a great mom, you already know. It was like that.

Abner

I'LL NEVER FORGET MY FIRST TRUE love. I was ready to propose early . . . too early, possibly. It's a story about a stubbed toe.

Did I have a ring?

No.

Did I have a plan?

Nope.

Did I have a job?

LOL.

Did she even know I liked her? Yeah, okay, so she didn't know that, either. I was convinced that this was true love, but I didn't act on anything yet. I was *determined,* though, that I would act on it . . . at some point.

The day finally came when I was going to let "my love" know about my intentions. I left the house, lunch in hand and a song humming in my chest. Mom kissed me on the cheek as I headed for another amazing day of fourth grade, where I sat behind the one and only Vivian Bass.

I stepped off the school bus, heart first, with a letter in hand that would make our future together clear to her. With anticipation so high my ears were ringing, I marched into Mr. Cue's classroom. My fourth-grade teacher was a renowned narcoleptic, so most of our in-class socializing happened in those two-minute spurts while he dozed. I

barely paid attention that day to anything other than the first signs of his head bobbing. The instant I saw him start his regular 11:00 A.M., first nod-off, I stepped out of my seat and stood next to Vivian Bass.

"I've got a letter for you," I said.

She looked up, confused.

She didn't hear me.

"I. Have. A. Letter for you," I sputtered a little too loudly, which got me hushed by the rest of the class, who were trying to enjoy a few minutes sans chaperone. I unwrinkled the communiqué balled up in my nervous fist and handed it over.

She read it aloud:

> "Dearest Vivian Bass.
>
> I love your name. I love your big eyes. I love your big ears and how they glow in the afternoon as the sun comes through the windows. I love you. We don't really talk much, but I know you love me, too. I'm having a birthday party in a couple weeks and I thought we could sneak into my mom's closet and kiss on the lips.
>
> Check yes or no.
>
> Abner"

The class was silent . . . for all of three seconds. Then *everyone* burst into laughter.

A red-faced Vivian Bass stood up, balled up my note, and threw it in the bin next to Mr. Cue's desk, at the very front of the room. The old war vet was shaking his brain back into alertness.

The rest of the day was a blur. An absolute blur. I was ruined. Devastated. Heart toyed with and shattered. Sure, we hadn't spoken to each other more than a dozen times. But *love is love,* man! I knew she felt it, too. She *had* to!

That night, Mom was making my fa-vorite meal, *ropa vieja,* for dinner. I was still on the couch crying my little nine-year-old eyes out when she called for me and my sisters to come eat. I made no such resolution to move. I lay there. I wept.

"Mijo, es tiempo de comer! Ven pa qua ahora!"

But, Mom! I'm brokenhearted. How can I possibly eat at a time like this?

What, even, was food? Why did I need to eat it? Everything was meaning-less in this void.

Everything except for . . . Vivian Bass.

Mom yelled at me again to come eat,

her tone making it clear that if she had to ask me one more time, I would regret it. I stood, in a huff. Angry, hurt, misunderstood. I stomped my way in the direction of the kitchen and—

Crack!

I'd stubbed my pinkie toe on the leg of the end table next to the couch. I recoiled from the deadly blow and loosed an anguished roar (really, I squeaked out an overblown sob, but a man has his pride). I fell onto the floor crying again, but for an entirely new reason. My foot felt like it was on fire, and it hurt to breathe.

It was all so clear. *This* was real pain. *This* was a good reason to cry. Maybe pain enlightens.

As Mom came to check on me, I finally spoke through the sobs.

"Why did I care so much about Vivian Bass?!"

• • •

Ten years later, when Amanda rolled her eyes at me in church, it wasn't that Vivian Bass pain. It was an end-table-cracking-your-toe type of enlightenment. In that moment I saw myself: *I'm at church just to mack on chicks.*

I realized that I had prioritized how I felt over who I felt I should be, that I had valued feeling good over being good.

Somehow, with the same passion of nine-year-old Abner, I knew this girl was more than just some prize. I also knew I needed to make some changes in myself. Very quickly, I discovered that all those years growing up in church had stuck with me more than I'd thought.

The day I saw Amanda was the beginning of a sacred revolution—the moment my faith became my own and not just an adopted belief system indoctrinated in me from birth. I realized that if something was worth believing, it was worth believing all the way.

I doubled down on the same church that I had been attending only for their, *cough,* "resources." I began helping with the middle and high school worship bands. I had certainly, after all, gotten my "ten thousand hours" in youth-band experience alone. Soon I found myself going on service trips to third-world countries, where I'd translate or sing or dig ditches or help build a roof. This honestly did more good for my soul than almost any service I'd ever sat through.

Four years went by like this, four years during which I never saw Amanda . . . at least not in person. I did, however, have a folder on my computer desktop, in my room, where I stored all the pictures of her I could find on the Internet just so I could stare at them. I called it the early version Google alerts, where I'd google her and alert myself to any new pictures of her that were available. She was modeling in New York City at the time, so it was pretty easy to get a steady stream of pics to load into my creeper vault. Full-on stalker status for your boy.

Along with leading high school worship and stalking New York models, I also managed to sign my first record deal and enter into my first lawsuit in those four years. *Yay me!*

I had so objectified the idea of signing a record deal that when my then manager (bless his heart) presented me with a deal from a local production company over dinner one night, I just signed it. No lawyer present, no days of negotiation, no actual wisdom involved. I looked over the thing once. I was nineteen and had zero experience. All I knew was that if I signed, I would be getting a new guitar and they'd pay a big down payment on a 2002 Volkswagen Golf. I had never owned an instrument and had played only on loaners from church when I was growing up, and I also had never owned a car. All I had to do was give up my rights to all intellectual property, to my likeness, to all masters of any musical creations, and agree to any other words they could make letters out of that stated some form of ownership over me. Again, all with no lawyer, no negotiating, and no experience.

Dear God.

They had me over a barrel showing me the fifty states. They had even asked my mom and dad to drive up from Florida to be there for the signing. At this signing, the head guy of the production company/ label/publishing company asked my dad to pray with him to bless the new deal. (Side note to artists: *Never* sign a deal with a company that wears all the hats. When they are a production company, label, *and* publishing company, it's just not in your favor, practically speaking, to sign with them. Yes, I'm looking at you, every-church-that-has-a-record-label.) We were in the head guy's office, where his desk sat on a real-life pedestal that set him eighteen inches higher than anyone else, with all the seats facing it having shortened legs, so you were always looking up at him while bringing your petitions to his throne. He also had lots of cutouts of gangster movies all around the room. Oof. The guy literally got on his knees in his office and asked my dad to follow suit, as he prayed a blessing over the deal. The dude wept, cried out to God, and fleeced me, all in the same breath. I signed the contract, forfeiting my next seven professional years.

· · ·

So there I was.

Did I have a career?

No.

I was Broke Phi Broke, running food out to tables and washing dishes at P.F. Chang's, unable to make music for a living because of a lawsuit over I-don't-even-remember-what.

Did I have a plan?

Nope.

I was back at church six times a week, along with digging ditches, building roofs, and singing for children in third-world countries anytime I got the chance.

Did I have doubts?

LOL.

Honestly, I'd never been happier.

It took Amanda and me years to realize something. A no often ends up being way more valuable than a yes. It's funny how life can work out like that.

When I first tried to make a move on Amanda, I received a resounding no. When the record deal I'd always wanted came along with a new car and new guitar, I couldn't help but respond with a big ole yes.

A bad yes is worse than a heartbreaking no, every day of the week.

The yes ended up being tragic, but the no turned out to be temporary. Eventually, that no became life-giving.

Amanda

IN THOSE FOUR YEARS BETWEEN seeing Abner and meeting him, a lot of life happened. Not just any old life, but that critical early-twenties life that feels heavy and important, because in so many ways it is. You're forging your own way, you're chasing dreams, you're becoming who you want to be, except you're not quite that person yet, and your brain isn't fully developed, so a lot of the time you're just straight-up guessing.

Along the way, I kept meeting people who had given up their passion for something more predictable. These people inadvertently gave me perseverance. They'd talk about their dreams more like a lover lost at sea than an ex they'd broken up with in an honest and mutual way. It's one thing to decide you want something different and another to give up on what you truly love. I hated the look of sadness and longing I'd always see in their eyes. I didn't want anyone to see that look in mine.

Fail, Amanda, fail, fail, and fail again, suck, be horrible, get rejected, try something new, suck some more, but don't give up. Just don't give up. Have a million side jobs to pay the bills. Do whatever you need to do, but keep your loves alive.

So I fumbled and wrote bad songs (I have a few I can show you) and worked with different producers and took guitar lessons. And, believe it or not, I even tried every now and again to sing for people in person. You'd think that as the daughter of two musicians I would know what I was doing. But the Internet made things weird in the music business at that time, so in some ways everyone was guessing just like I was. All I really did was whatever I could. That's it. No plan. Just a lot of recording myself and my horrible guitar playing in GarageBand.

Luckily, I didn't have to worry too much about a job. A few months before moving to New York, I had visited my sister, Brooklyn, there, who at the time was pursuing acting by way of commercial modeling. She needed to drop something off at her agency, Ford Models, a staple in the modeling world. I walked in with her, feeling crazy insecure and wondering who could do this for a job—only to be judged by appearance day in and day out, never eating french fries and having to spend conscious effort on not being bloated. Oof. Nightmare, right?

I assumed her agent was going to be a pushy douche, and I braced myself as I walked into his office. Instead, I met one of the kindest, gentlest, sweetest souls: Ray Volant. We hit it off, and suddenly I understood why my sister actually liked this commercial-modeling thing so much.

A few weeks later, Ray called and asked if I wanted to sign with the new agency he was starting, Bella Agency. I unleashed all my worries on him over the phone, including but not limited to my feeling fat and ugly, not wanting to work out, fear of rejection, boredom while waiting at go-sees (very on-the-nose industry term for an audition), and not having time for my passions, which included music and the aforementioned french fries. He and his partner, Susan, encouraged me to get past my preconceived notions and fears, and they explained the concept of residuals: the money you get paid every time a commercial you star in airs. Um, say what?? Free money?! Where do I sign? Suddenly excited and fear free, I went to my first appointment. It was for a Subway commercial. I booked it.

Soon after, I met a guy and we started dating. He was what I like to call a "real" model, meaning he came to New York to do this one thing—he focused on it, succeeded at it, and had career goals. He also had 4 percent body fat. I had no such thing. I had the desire to pay some bills and spend my time elsewhere. Even though at the core we were very different people, we hit it off and kept each other

CHILL
BABE!
—Abner

company for a few years. We had a good thing going, and for much of the time, I thought he was it. The one. We were pretty serious, or at least I thought we were for a while.

But something kept me hesitant. Something kept me going back to Nashville. Nashville was the polar opposite of New York in so many ways. New York had action and a sexy sort of loneliness, crowded streets, and the energy that comes from a few million people on one small island hustling their butts off to succeed. There was the possibility of fairy tales coming true around each corner, and grocery stores that were more like a food hoarder's pantry than a store. It had magic, but it was hard.

Nashville, on the other hand, had community and stillness, open fields and creativity that comes from people who love their craft and would do it every day passionately even if no one ever recognized them or payed any attention. It was easy and stable and, most of all, Nashville had Publix, an organized, well-lit, spacious grocery store with everything you could need, at a decent price.

Glory to God, Publix was enough to make me move back. I missed it and needed a break from the big city. New York had started to wear on me, a fact I didn't want to admit, and so did the rela-

tionship I was in, also a fact I didn't want to admit. Neither was a good fit for me anymore. So I flew home for Easter, tired and in need of novel inspiration. That was the night I met Abner. It was March 15, 2005. I know that was the date, because I just googled it. How romantic.

• • •

A fellow songwriter actually helped bring us together. Mat Kearney was an old friend of mine, and he just so happened to be Abner's roommate. On that fateful March night, we all wound up in line together at a small but lively coffee shop known for staying open twenty-four hours a day.

After all those years of my actively avoiding him, there we were, standing next to each other and staring at the menu. I was still technically taken, so I didn't feel the urge to run from him or hide anymore. Plus, my emotional maturity had finally reached a place higher than a nine-year-old schoolgirl's. Praise be. I remember I was wearing low-waisted, flared jeans covered with tears and patches. I thought they were so cool, so I was feeling pretty confident that night. Come to find out, in hindsight, they were horrible and ugly and I probably should have been embarrassed, a truth that revealed itself to me as years passed. Abner, I'm pretty sure, was

wearing his belt buckle off to one side and maybe even had a pager attached, so bless us both and our early 2000s fashion sense. No one was safe back then.

It felt so strange to be standing in front of this guy, who had caused me so much anxiety in years past, and not be looking for an emergency exit. Even stranger was how kind and charming he was. For years I had imagined an over-confident player, the kind of guy you'd be super into while also being aware the whole time he was an emotional dumpster fire luring you into his abyss. Turns out, he wasn't any of those things. He was sweet and gracious and just the right amount of confident (okay, fine, maybe just slightly overconfident).

"I've been wanting to meet you for years," Abner said.

Oh, crap.

There went my heart, slowly slipping through my fingers with one sentence.

Who knows how I replied, but from what I can tell I got out a halfway normal sentence, paid for my coffee, and then went to sit down with the friend I was there to meet up with. Not long after-ward, Abner found me again. "Is it okay if I come sit with you?" he asked.

Yeah sure yeah sure yeah yeah sure sure no big deal sure yeah that's fine, I'm chill whatever.

CHILL BABE! —Abner

49

He sat down nonchalantly with my friend and me, speaking to us like we were both old beloved friends, disarming me with ease. After five minutes, several of my single friends received a text exclaiming I had met the most incredible guy and I would be actively trying to set one of them up. He was the catch of a lifetime. It took me no time to see that. Oof, I just wanted to be around him, but I had that whole boyfriend/career thing in another city so I knew he couldn't be for me. Still, I reveled in our new friendship and the official end to my Abner Ramirez strike.

I left Nashville inspired, because maybe I couldn't be with Abner, but just knowing that guys like him existed changed my perspective. Suddenly I knew I had been building a life in New York that was less and less mine. It was the life I was supposed to want, the life a younger version of myself thought she needed. But Abner, literally in a matter of minutes, showed me everything I actually wanted. He was a real person, grounded and present, talented but not consumed with it, charming but not an ounce fake. He loved music and people, and was happy to be a busboy if it meant he got to enjoy those things and do what he loved. There was infinite passion without the nagging pressure that often accompanies it.

We kept in touch via a really cool new music–centered social media platform called Myspace (yes, we put each other on our Top 8's). I was about to turn twenty-three and was starting to piece together a clearer vision of what I hoped my life could be. As much as I tried to make it work, New York fit the picture less and less. And, strangely, this guy I had met once and my old hometown of Nashville fit it more and more.

After a few months of indecision, I cut ties with my boyfriend and my city, then booked a flight back home. Abner, noticing I was in town thanks to social media, invited me to a show he was playing at a small club called 12th & Porter, the club that later played host to the first ever JOHNNYSWIM show. He played with all the dynamic charisma he's now known for, and I'm sure I wasn't the only one in the room who felt he was singing directly to them. Great artists do that, but as he played, I grew more and more overwhelmed. I couldn't tell if I wanted to marry him, write with him, sing like him, maybe just *be* him. I had all the feels, all at once. Something was happening.

Good thing my New York boyfriend and I had broken up a few months before, because It. Was. On!

51

GOOD THING MY N[

NO. ON!

IT. WAS. IT. WAS.

BEFORE. BECAUSE

Abner

I don't want to see
The shining sun
Or the moon.
Neither do I want to contemplate
Millions of romantic stars.
All I want to see
Is your smile,
And it will make my day bright.

IT'S HARD TO READ THIS POEM excerpt written by my father. It's probably always gonna hurt a little when I hear his voice on a recording or video. But reading his poetry is like hearing him right there in the room. It will always make me feel like he's right there with me. Thick Cuban accent, bad grammar, and all. His absence is too fresh a wound . . . and maybe always will be. When Dad was a pastor, it was my mom, Marisol, who would sing and play the piano at church, leading the congregation in song. She still sings and plays beautifully (she's *way* too humble to be comfortable reading that. Oh well. Learn to take a compliment, Mom!). While Marisol sang and played with grace, my dad couldn't carry a tune in a bucket, but for some reason, his was always the loudest voice in the room.

Omar Ramirez may have been tone-deaf, but he was an incredible writer. Most of his poems were written in Spanish and had a common theme: They were either poems about Mom, or they were poems about Cuba. Dad would write about Cuba like it was a lover he'd lost. One year right before Christmas, I told my father that all I wanted from him were copies of his poetry. So he headed to Kinko's and printed them out for me as a gift. It was the beginning of a tradition he kept up for every birthday and holiday every year from then until his passing.

The poems are often about his childhood. They reflect how my family came to America, a story he told me one thousand three hundred eighty-six times. But those tales never grew old. I haven't read them in a long time. I'm a 7 on the Enneagram: I tend to run from that kind of pain.

It's impossible for me to adequately tell the whole story. In truth, my father's journey deserves its own book. So instead, I'll try to give you a glimpse. Just like a poem might.

> I don't want to conquer
> Lands or kingdoms
> Neither the outer space.
> I don't want the glory
> Of any king.
> All I want to have
> Is a place in your life
> And be the king of your heart.

It's April 1980, and things in Cuba are a mess. The beautiful revolution of the people that so many had received with open arms just a couple of decades before is rotting the island from the inside out. At the time, a family of four is given about one pound of meat to survive on for ten to fifteen days. Sometimes that pound of "meat" is actually just bones with a little something attached. Doctors moonlight as taxi drivers to earn enough money to support their families (a fact that remains true today). Outspoken rivals of the revolution are imprisoned or murdered with no evidence set against them.

With anti-revolutionary sentiment in the country bubbling to overflowing,

55

the Peruvian embassy is offering asylum to about ten thousand Cubans. A block away, my dad and his younger brother discuss with their wives the possibility of getting into the embassy and leaving Cuba. The line to get in is a mile long (literally), and those waiting have to endure the verbal and physical abuse of members of the Cuban government and its sympathizers.

Organized religion has become the number one enemy of the state. Anything that can rally the people en masse is bad news, and religion is something Cubans hold in higher regard than they do the government. So religion is about to become government controlled or abolished altogether. Because of this, my father, a pastor, is under constant threat of being sent to a labor camp. His brother-in-law is also a pastor and was arrested in his home and sent to work at a UMAP labor camp for a year—just for being a Christian. My mother is a brilliant student, having studied physics at the University of Havana for two years, before she is informed that she won't be able to become the physics professor she has aspired to be. This also is due to the fact that she is a Christian. As such, she is not allowed to teach.

My dad is a freaking wild card. He pastors three different churches in and around Havana—the largest boasting

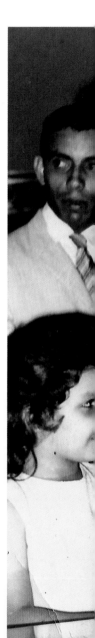

two hundred members—just when the laws are becoming more and more stringent about what a pastor is allowed to say from the pulpit. Omar Ramirez is a street kid too passionate to let simple threats of violence and incarceration dissuade him from his purpose. He serves these communities not just through his sermons but with his life: building roofs, counseling families. He will literally get in the fight right next to you if you need him to.

He always was my kind of pastor.

One week, the government establishes a law that forbids a pastor from saying that Fidel Castro needs Jesus in order to get to Heaven. That very weekend, my dad hangs a banner in front of the largest church he pastors in Havana: IF FIDEL DOESN'T REPENT AND PROCLAIM JESUS AS LORD, HE WILL BURN IN HELL FOR ETERNITY.

Many pastors are snatched silently in the middle of the night and taken to labor camps, where they will languish for years, for far less dramatic prose than my father's. But my father has earned the right to speak out. He's garnered the support and love of the community through his service and strong, no-nonsense speech. The government can't do anything too overt to him or they will make him a hero in death. They don't want to make him a martyr. So they leave him alone, at least in the obvious ways.

But they find other ways to threaten him: Like, when he's out walking with his family, cars *often* swerve off the road, just narrowly missing him, his wife, and two baby girls. Obviously, he's being followed. They know his every move.

Then there's the time my father is out walking near a school in Havana and hears a familiar voice coming from the speakers of the school. When he recognizes the voice, his walk turns into a run. My middle sister, Litka, is being made to read the Communist creed in front of the whole school, a creed declaring the *patria* (country) over all religions, over even blood family. He runs into the school, onto the stage, and takes Litka home.

That same year, my oldest sister, Abdi, is in class when the teacher asks if anybody in the class has been going to church. Only Abdi raises her hand. The teacher begins to insult and berate her, making enough of a spectacle of my sister for the entire class to laugh at her as she covers her face and runs home.

With repressive conditions like these, barely enough food to eat, and no road to opportunity outside of working for the Communist party, my dad knows it's time for a change. This *revolución* "of the people" oppresses all people except the powerful. It mocks the heart, thoughts, and opinions of all but the cowed. Families like mine, with outlying foundation-al beliefs, become outcasts. They have to leave Cuba.

> I don' need all the knowledge
> Of letters and science
> That makes you respected
> and famous.
> I don't need the money
> That makes a man powerful.
> All I need to know, honey,
> Is that you're in love with me,
> And my life will be wonderful.

Okay. I swear I'm trying to tell this story quickly, but it's just so damn crazy. Let's fast-forward just a bit.

By May 1980, things are even more tense on the Pearl of the Caribbean. President Jimmy Carter sees how the people of Cuba are suffering and starving. How they are risking their lives on ninety-mile inner-tube rides across the sea just to get to America, and spending their last drop of energy trying to dodge border patrols. All this . . . just for a *chance* to live in freedom. So Carter declares that the USA will accept any Cuban immigrants who have family stateside to receive them.

Castro begrudgingly agrees, knowing that if he gets these "traitors" out of his country, the infighting and whatnot will be easier to contain. The expectations are

for ten thousand people to make this trip. (There are many details of this story I'm leaving out—I'll have to save them for a later, longer version.) Instead, eventually one hundred thousand Cubans make the ninety-mile journey through a hurricane to America in what becomes known as the Mariel Boatlift. To freedom. This number doesn't include the thousands who will die along the way. (Did I mention that Castro held them at port for days, only to send them out during a hurricane?!)

As the rescue boats arrive at the harbor in Cuba, each family waiting to be picked up runs the risk of being beaten or thrown into jail for being a traitor. They have had to sneak out of their homes with nothing but what they are wearing—with no money, no keepsakes, no change of clothes.

Around ten years before this, my dad's oldest brother, Efrain Ramirez, had claimed asylum in Spain and worked his way to U.S. citizenship. Now, when my dad tells him that he's bringing his family to the United States, my uncle Efrain and two other families pool their money to rent a boat, a twenty-three-footer named *The Adenike,* to collect their families. They are going to take the United States–sanctioned opportunity to travel ninety miles from Key West in *The Adenike* to snatch up their twenty-two relatives

59

awaiting them in Cuba and then head back to Key West. Should take a day. Maybe two. *Max.*

So. Many. Details. Go. Here.

My father, mother, and two older sisters sneak out of their home one day, taking with them exactly what the other refugees have: nothing. Nothing but hope, the hope that however hard it might be to get to the next place, that next place will be worth it. They make the trek to the beach with other members of our family—fifteen people, including six children under nine years old. This includes a six-year-old, a seven-year-old, and two grandmothers, all sleeping on the sand, exposed to the elements, for five days. People outside the beach throw rocks and eggs at the "traitors," whom the throwers believe are ridiculous for wanting to leave. Oh, and the people sleeping on the sand can't touch the water or leave the beach, so their toilet is wherever they dig a hole . . . unavoidably near the other few thousand folks on the same beach.

After five days, my family is finally moved to the port of Mariel, where their boats await them for departure. All are desperate to get off the island and head to a place where they can make choices for themselves and their family. There are supposed to be only 22 people boarding *The Adenike,* but instead more than 130 people climb aboard.

It turns out the government decided to load more than a hundred grown men from the maximum-security prison and the insane asylum onto the boat that my uncle and two other families rented for a rescue mission, all to be loosed onto the streets of America.

Anyhoo . . . super cheerful story, so I'll keep it shortish.

My family and the others end up being held at port for three more days before being told they have to leave, just as a hurricane is approaching. Many boats experience engine failure. *The Adenike* ends up towing a boat loaded with folks for a full day until the rope snaps. Everybody aboard the other boat dies at sea.

See? Cheerful!

My family arrives at Key West on June 6, 1980. Their lives are forever changed.

I will never have to know what it is like fighting for my dreams in such a literal way, as my family did in Cuba. I am born three years later, in 1983, in Jacksonville, Florida, a city that cost my family everything to get to.

> And when my life runs to the end,
> I don't fear crossing the river
> Or all the struggles and pain.
> I don't care about losses or gain.
> I want your farewell with a smile.
> Please, don't drop any tears.
> All I fear is that I'm going to a place,
> Where to see you again,
> I'll just have to wait.

—Omar Ramirez

Amanda

WELL . . . THAT WAS AN INTENSE story, so I'll chill things out a bit.

After living alone in New York during those few years, I moved back to Nashville, desperate to be near songwriters and artists who weren't overly concerned with success—folks who were in it for the love of creating. And I wanted an intentional community of friends. At first, I traveled back and forth to New York for work. But eventually I got a job at a Starbucks in Nashville and traded go-sees for making lattes. The pay and prestige were far less as a barista, but hey, it was worth it. I'd come to see that living in New York was like building a house in a tornado, frantic and desperate. Nashville was slow. I had more control to create the life I wanted with the people I wanted, who included a very handsome musician named Abner Ramirez.

Abner and I hit it off immediately. Rumors flew early and often about us dating, which, like all good young Christian singles, we denied or ignored until it was just plain dumb. Denial for me came easily, though, because anytime Abner asked me out, he also invited around 60 to 70 percent of all the other people he had ever met. Nothing has changed. He still loves a party. It's simultaneously my favorite and least favorite of his spiritual

gifts. Favorite, because he builds community and culture so beautifully, with sincerity and ease. Least favorite, because date nights get a little crowded and less intimate when fourteen people tag along.

I appreciated those early and frequent group hangs, but they gave me little insight into whether my feelings for Abner were reciprocated. Most of you haven't met him, so let me tell you again . . . the guy is charming. Super charming. To everyone. To your grandma. The mailman. Your second cousin. The shy girl. The creepy guy. The hostess and the busboy. The president of the company running an event and the janitor waiting for the room to clear so he can clean up and go home. I saw his charm that first night at the coffee shop and I still see it every dang day. Abner is an equal-opportunity offender with his innate magnetism and kindness. He can't be any other way. He probably came out of the womb waving and saying hello to the doctor and nurses, thanking them for their hard work and wishing them a great evening: "You guys are the best in the world! You did great getting me out of there."

It's really just who he is. It's wonderful and honest and so sweet. But this charm plus his affinity for large-group gatherings did little Amanda no favors. If you're a young twentysomething girl hoping this guy likes you, you will be very confused. You will doubt every romantic word he says to you, every flirtatious gesture, and ultimately not pick up on any of the clues he thinks he's obviously dropping. You will look clueless, because, in fact, you are. He and his universal charisma have left you no choice but to be ignorant of his love for you.

Which is why on one chilly September evening, I didn't notice the extra hint of excitement in his voice when he called me from work. I could hear plates *clink* in the background. I assumed the nerves I heard in his voice were just your run-of-the-mill "I'm not supposed to be on the phone during work" nerves. I thought nothing of it. He asked if I'd want to meet him for a movie when his shift ended. I gave him a quick, enthusiastic yes. *Sure! Sounds like another great group activity.* It didn't dawn on me that this might be a different type of invitation, one with a different intention than usual. I prepped for the night like I would any other night . . . by not prepping. I wore whatever I happened to be wearing that day, and made zero extra effort before leaving the house, unless you count applying deodorant as extra.

On my way to the theater, Abner called to tell me he had unexpectedly gotten off work early and was waiting at the theater

67

for me with our tickets. *Wait, what?* My ears and heart perked up. He had never bought my movie ticket before. The bells in my head started slowly ringing. Was this about to be a . . . date?! Should I have dressed up? Why didn't I think this through? Big mistake. Huge!

Before I could stop myself, I blurted out a question I had asked him so many times before but realized later was ill advised for this particular evening: "Who else is coming?"

Crickets . . . He was silent. He then quickly mumbled something about not being sure, and got off the phone with lightning speed.

Uh-oh.

I called my friend Holly immediately to discuss my suspicions. After a quick tutorial from her on how to put on a full face of makeup with a tube of Chapstick, a cheek slap, and a prayer, I scooted into the theater, whisper-screaming into my phone as I shoved it into my purse that I would text her soon with updates. I was nervous. I was excited. I was . . . wrong.

Waiting for me near the concessions stood Abner, right next to his old roommate Michael Cantrell.

Wow. I tried to act unsurprised. Not only was this not a date, but I was basically crashing their guy hang. My only hope now was that we would sit next to

each other and maybe, just maybe, be like middle schoolers and hold hands with sweaty palms for the first time. I wouldn't grieve my hopes just yet.

We found a good open row in the center of the theater, and Abner, being a gentleman, motioned for me to choose my seat first. Then, in a move I think surprised even him, he motioned for his roommate to go down the aisle next. So there we were, for three hours in the dark: me, then Michael, then Abner, staring at the screen in a very non-date-like way, yet again confirming I couldn't read this guy at all. I went to the bathroom and texted Holly.

Not a date. (Single-tear emoji.)

I had never been well versed in romance, but Abner fully perplexed me. I could not figure him out. He was simultaneously mysterious and transparent. I hadn't met anyone like him. Still haven't. Every time we talked, I learned something new about him. Things that most guys would serve up on a silver platter, Abner never mentioned until they came up naturally. Like the fact he grew up playing violin. That's a hella sexy quality, let's be honest. But for months he never said a word about it. When it came up in the car one night, I thought he was joking. Then he pulled into his driveway, walked into his garage, and whipped out

a violin. He played a piece that made me want to cry, then nonchalantly tossed the violin aside and walked inside the house, unfazed. He wasn't being cocky, nor was he being shy. He just didn't try to woo me with extras. They wouldn't have held up anyway.

He wooed me with his authenticity and the character he'd spent the last few years working on. The more his character unfolded, the more it thrilled me. Before I knew it, my daydreams featured fully formed wedding vignettes.

Sadly, things kept on as usual for a few more weeks after our nondate. We rolled into October still hanging with a gang of friends as if nothing had happened or had almost happened. No middle school handholding ever occurred. At times I thought I was making it all up.

Then, one day Abner called with an invitation to dinner. Just like before, his voice was a little nervous, and just like before, he received a quick yes from me.

Having learned from my previous mistakes, I prepared myself, in case this night was different: real makeup, real deodorant, and an actual outfit. I probably even put on too much Clinique Happy, just for good measure. I called Holly, just like before, as I approached the restaurant, hoping she could calm my nerves and help me steel myself for what might be another disappointment.

The restaurant was noisy. A crowd of at least twenty people were spilling into the parking lot, waiting for tables. I didn't see Abner outside or just inside the doors at the hostess stand, so I went in and carefully scanned the room. Holding the phone to my face, I crouched down angling myself just right so I could see around folks and into the dining room. Anticipation mounted. Holly squealed in my ear unable to handle the suspense anymore. I found a good spot behind a large gentleman to stake out the room. I needed to get a glimpse of him before he got one of me, so I could prepare my own reaction. I had a lot riding on this night!

Finally, I saw Abner standing in the corner, waving to get my attention. He had found me despite my excellent hiding spot. "Oh crap, Holly, I've got to go." I hung up before she could fully respond, slamming my flip phone shut as the words "Is he alone?" screamed through the receiver. I took a deep breath, trying to look cool as I made my way around busy tables toward him. He welcomed me with a smile and his signature Abner hug. The jitters left my gut. Butterflies repacked them. I smiled and hugged him a little extra tight.

He was at a table for two.

Abner

THE NIGHT WE MET AT THE COFFEE shop was probably one of the best moments of my life. I was so happy to see Amanda, and I had grown enough in the four years since I'd first seen her to be happy just to be in her presence. I knew real quick that I would eagerly be in her life in any capacity that she would have me. I'd get friend-zoned with a smile, if it meant being near her. (That sounds sweet, and I honestly felt that way back then. But it just sounds like the *absolute worst* now.) I knew she was going back and forth to NYC at that point, and I had a show coming up at 12th & Porter in Nashville. . . .

Okay, wait a minute. . . . Let's scratch that paragraph. This is beginning to sound like a Hallmark movie. It's a lot deeper than that.

Let's not start with drinking coffee and swapping stories. Let's start with diving into deep waters and sharing your soul.

• • •

To reach into the abyss with both hands —expectant, dependent, and hopeful— then pull your hands back out holding something you hope is beautiful but often is not: That's songwriting to me. Sometimes it's more like jumping headfirst into that abyss blindfolded, desperate, scared, and losing your patience—still hopeful, but stitched more with desperation than confidence.

Risk. Expectation. Hope. In my opinion, that's the recipe. That's what it takes every time to get where you want to go.

Some of our fans' favorite songs almost didn't make it into our repertoire. "Annie," "Adelina," and other songs that don't start with the letter A (but I believe in alliteration) almost weren't finished just because they were *hard* to finish. It's a wild ride to write songs when they come tumbling out of you with a nonstop surge of inspiration. It's easy, in those moments, to believe that's the way songwriting *should* feel. It's legit addicting to, almost accidentally, have a song come out of you from a depth and honesty that leaves you discovering how you *truly* feel about something like love, death, or a milkshake. You hear words forged out of feelings and coming out of you unbridled, mounted onto melody. But some songs take longer to come to life. Instead of arriving in a surge of inspiration, they're marked by long pauses in the writing session where we just sort of wait for them to interrupt our daydreaming.

We sit, hoping that we can substitute an actual song for the lists we were silently making of jobs we were better qualified for than songwriting. This process can take days, months, or years to finally arrive at a finished product if you have the patience to wait for the songs to come to life. But, man, what a lesson, to see those songs finally form after their having been on life support for so long.

Those painful births sometimes lead to unexpected blessings. We get emails and DMs all the time about newborn babies named Adelina, and we've had some of our heroes of songwriting tell us how great a song "Annie" is.

I'll never forget the time Vince Gill pulled us to the side in the wings of the stage at the Ryman to tell us what he thought of "Annie": "That song is great." Spoken in very Vince form, with no dramatic flourishes, just honest and to the point. When we didn't really respond, he grabbed my arm and pulled me closer. "I mean it, man. That song is good. Like Simon and Garfunkel good."

Okay, so maybe Vinnie *is* given to little bouts of flourish here and there, but I tell you what—I'll live the rest of my life with a crystal-clear picture of him saying that to us. I wish I could hang that memory on my wall or forge it into a trophy. Dang. Feels so good just to relive it right

now. Writing those songs felt hopeless at times. I'm glad for the clarity of hindsight. It teaches me that a thing doesn't have to feel like magic at its inception to be magical at its core.

Abner and Amanda are a song that almost didn't happen. One that ended up being pretty damn great, too. It wasn't easy, but the recipe felt familiar: Risk. Expectation. Hope.

• • •

Okay, so I've already admitted to the whole light cyber-stalker thing. But a thing I haven't mentioned yet is that I had a friend named Smoothes who was equally obsessed with Amanda's sister, Brooklyn. (His story didn't turn out like mine.) We'd sit up in my room comparing pictures of Amanda and Brooklyn we found online and arguing over who was hotter. *Ha! Why am I admitting this?*

A few weeks after finally meeting Amanda in person, at the coffee shop, I invited her (over Myspace) to come see me perform an opening set at 12th & Porter. Her response, "Maybe." So, clearly, I had to call Smoothes and brag that Amanda Grace Sudano was absolutely, definitely, sure-as-the-sun-rises-in-the-east, coming to my show. We

HOME

- "ALL POSE" BRK DWN
- LAST "ALL BRUSED" BRING BLU'S IN ON
"ONLY LOVE WILL MAKE YOU UNDERSTAND" & OUT
ON "COLD ME SOME"
- BREAKDOWN 2ND OR 3RD VERSE
- TAKE CLAPS OUT ON "HOME" & BRING BACK ON
AFTER "COLD ME SOME HOME"

DELINA

- GIT @ 28 SLOPPY (27-28)
- TAKE LEAD HIT OUT OF CHORUSES

HOME NEW

AUX: GIT: -1.3
      Vox: -5.2

- TAKE OUT MEASURES 33-38
- BLEND GITS @ 75
- CATCH GIT (BREAK) @ 29 LEAD IN TO V2

both knew I was being ridiculous, and we laughed it off.

The night of the show came. I was doing my pre-performance ritual of hanging with the same six of my friends who came to all my gigs because they were kind and had nothing better to do. As we waited for the show to start, I saw Smoothes turn his head to the entrance and then look back at me with full-on red-alert eyes. You know, like there was an earthquake and we had only seconds to act. The conversation in our small group was cut off as Smoothes marched straight through our circle and grabbed me by both shoulders, dragging me off a few feet while never breaking eye contact with me. It felt strangely like a really intense dance (a tough move to pull off naturally, but we called him Smoothes for a reason).

He took a couple of breaths before speaking. "Abner . . . you need to know this before you go up there tonight . . . Amanda Sudano is here . . . Amanda Grace Sudano is here tonight to see you sing . . . *Don't mess this up.*"

Yep. Definitely an earthquake.

(Years later when Amanda and I were making our late-night television debut on *The Tonight Show with Jay Leno,* I remember hearing Leno introducing us: " *. . . their late-night- television debut, please welcome Johnny . . .* " As the curtains were being raised, I bellowed, in full voice, to the band, *"Don't mess this up!"* I guess that's what we say now when we're really nervous.)

Growing up in church, and especially being in the worship band, we often talked about singing "to an audience of one." No matter how many people were in the room, our mind's attention and heart's affection should be directed to God Himself. God forgive me, but that term took on a new meaning for me that night. Certainly, my mind and heart were attuned. Just, uh . . . not to Him.

I've never been more nervous to play four songs. As the opening act, I didn't get to play long, didn't get paid, and usually just hoped the headliner brought enough people that I'd get a chance to make new fans. Tonight . . . Amanda Grace Sudano was there . . . to see me sing.

I don't remember anything about my performance. Next thing I knew, I was at the bar. I do remember having snuck around backstage to get there. I had almost figured out whether I was there to celebrate or to sulk just when she sat down next to me.

"So, what are you doing with this music thing?" the angel said.

"I signed a bad record deal once, so I'm never going to pursue music as a career again," the ogre responded.

"Well, that's stupid."

Was the angel mocking me??

"We should write," she said.

"Uh, what?" I philosophized.

"Let's write. Here's my number. Let's make it happen."

The order was certainly one I would obey.

The first time we wrote a song together was a few months after our meeting. It was magic from the start, and it had nothing to do with songwriting. She showed up at the house I was sharing with two roommates from church, one being Mat Kearney, the fellow songwriter who introduced us.

I remember opening the door, stunned.

Her: red summer dress, flawless white teeth showing behind a warm smile, sun-kissed skin, smooth and perfect hair in sync with the breeze moving along to some unheard song from Heaven.

Me: unbathed, unlaundered, teeth still wearing their morning sweaters at noon, feet exposed and fully ashy to the knee.

The song we wrote was fine. We sang it for years, and maybe we'll sing it again someday (it was called "Letting Go," and had a cool F#7 chord in it). But I couldn't have cared less about the song at the time. Thank God for the Internet, patience, perfect timing, and my boys, Smoothes and Mat Kearney, or we never would've even gotten this far.

The *moment,* and I mean this, the *moment* we started singing together, I felt like a hive of flying baby unicorns were born in my belly. Listen, I would've sat with her to watch paint dry if she wanted. I'd been pseudo-stalking this chick for *years.* But she wanted to write a song together, and we sounded *good* together. There was no reason not to do this more often, right? Every week, maybe? Every day? For like, the rest of our lives? *I'm down if you are.*

Risk.

Expectation.

And after that first time writing and singing together? A *whole lot* of hope.

Amanda

WHEN I WAS A KID, ALL I WANTED to do was perform. It's the only thing I ever dreamt of doing (except for the years I wanted to be a singer who also played in the WNBA, but that was a short-lived aspiration). This was an unlikely dream to have, because I wasn't just shy; I was woefully insecure and refused to perform for anyone for any reason. I had no right and no reason to want a career in entertainment.

But look at me now! That's showbiz, babe! That's showbiz. Life is full of so much irony.

Maybe the passion for music was just in my blood. Obviously, growing up in a house of musicians nudged me in this direction to some degree. My parents were always the first to encourage creativity, even to a fault. If it was raining outside and my sister and I were bored and looking to whine a bit about it, my parents would recommend we write a song. We'd roll our eyes. *Can't we just complain about being bored for a while?* But we usually did it. Then if we were lucky, my dad would take us to his studio to record what we had written. Somewhere in a box in a Nashville basement is a cassette tape of the five-year-old me singing the new single "My Teacher Gave Me a Star on My

Work Today." It was a heartfelt tune, but unfortunately, no part of it rhymed and the melody lacked flair.

Honestly, though, I spent a lot of time not feeling good enough . . . not talented enough, not skilled enough, not interesting enough. I didn't sound like my mom or my sisters, or like Jodi Benson. (Anyone else have a childhood obsession with her? No? Just me? Cool. Look her up; you probably did.) I used to think I needed the right vocal coach or technique or song to make me great or the right person to develop me into something that could wow. Once I had that, I would take the stage. What stage, you ask? The one that would magically appear in front of thousands as soon as I was ready. I would then blow everyone away with my undeniable talent, cultivated privately over all the previous years. This was the only way I saw things working. I had no desire to learn in front of others, nor did I have the balls to fail in public. It's amazing I ever took a first step.

By the time I was a teenager, I had started compiling a list of my great inspirations. Not just of the artists whose work I loved, but ones who helped me to see myself, who I was and who I wanted to be creatively. The first, Bob Dylan, was

an epiphany. He sounded like only himself and told stories I could see. He gave me hope that greatness doesn't always sound or look or talk the same. He gave me some chutzpah to be myself.

Then, the summer before my junior year in high school, we traveled across Europe by rental car with my parents. Lauryn Hill had just come out with *The Miseducation of Lauryn Hill,* and that was it. That record was the only thing I listened to the whole trip. My parents were probably hoping for some good quality time on those long drives, but I was having quality time with those songs. They were just so honest. They weren't formulaic or typical. They made me feel like I knew her and at the same time made me feel known.

By the end of that summer, I was all in. I wasn't trying to be perfect anymore. I wanted vulnerability. I wanted honesty. I wanted to write and sing like I was born to, not like I was meant to. I had zero clue what the first step would be, but it didn't matter. I was already in the air leaping forward.

Abner

"I'M NOT GOING TO WALK AT GRAD-
uation," I said one night over dinner.

It was my senior year of high school, and I had to tell my parents the truth.

My dad didn't believe it. "Not true," he said.

"No, Dad, I'm not lying. I got a D-minus in American History, and I can't walk at graduation."

"Fix it. You're walking."

Welp.

At the time, I was going to an *amazing* art school, Douglas Anderson School of the Arts. I had had pretty good grades up until my senior year. Having transferred in from an academic magnet school, I got to choose how many academic classes I wanted to take, as long as I received at least the state minimum requirement of academic credits. The fewer academic classes I took, the more time I got to spend in my music classes. But it certainly caused added pressure on me to get a decent grade in every academic class I took. I was a violinist in the chamber orchestra, and I got to sit in with the jazz band and take extra music theory and music history classes. So, obviously, I took as few academic classes as possible with the caveat that I had to at least get a C in every academic class to graduate. Okay,

I'll fast-forward . . . I clearly *did not* meet the state minimum requirement of academic credits, because I got a D-minus in a history class.

In my defense, the teacher hated me.

In his defense, I cheated on every test and copied all my homework from someone else the period before his class.

I was coasting through my senior year academically, while absolutely *living* for my music classes. My history teacher made a point to be the one to tell me that I would not be graduating and would need to spend my summer retaking history class . . . with him. He assured me that there would be so few students in the class that I would be seated too far away from other students to copy their answers.

Long story longer: My advisor at school *loved* me. Instead of making me retake the history class, she got me into a class at a community college near my house, where I spent the last two weeks of high school retaking a year's worth of American History.

I cheated on every test, and copied all my homework. I got a B-plus.

I couldn't help but feel like I'd beaten the system the night I walked across the stage to get my diploma with my classmates. The law that had allowed me this

escape hatch was subsequently changed in Duval County that summer, preventing any future student from the last-minute panic-victory I'd managed to finagle. The new law was petitioned for very strongly by an incredibly angry, red-faced American History teacher, who resigned the day after my graduation.

I got a scholarship to FSU in Tallahassee to play in the orchestra, and was all set up to start my freshman year there. But, boy, did I want to get out of Flor-

ida. I had no idea how to start a career in music, but other than Lynyrd Skynyrd and Limp Bizkit, there weren't really any local bands from Jacksonville that had "made it." I realized my first step had to be getting out of there (or writing my own version of "Nookie"). I knew I needed to move somewhere that had a legitimate music scene. There were really only three options: New York, Los Angeles, and Nashville. But we were a poor immigrant family, and even though I did great

on standardized testing and had a great-looking after-school service report, I *barely* graduated from high school. It didn't look like I had a whole lot of options.

I remember the day Dad dropped me off in front of the orchestra building at FSU for freshman orientation, to let me head in and get settled while he looked for parking. As I walked through the building's front door, it felt like I was choking, like I couldn't catch any air. It felt like in that one moment, the entirety of my life was charted out before me. What was most obvious on that map of practicality and "wise decision-making," glaring with a brilliance I couldn't ignore, was just how much I would have to settle, how much I would be giving up. With this first step into FSU, I would be solidifying a course that would at best be shades of gray—I'd find a great job and a house near my parents that I'd likely never leave.

Dreams not dashed, just left unpursued. Which was worse. I knew it was time to make a leap of faith. One that, for me, didn't start in Tallahassee.

I built up the courage to tell Dad the truth: I couldn't move to campus and spend my next four years in a city where I would just gather debt and no better start in the career I wanted than on the west side of Jacksonville.

I decided I would just come right out and tell him. I had a plan: *I'll get a job and work hard. I'll convince him I'm right. I'll say all the right things. And by no means will I chicken out and make up some terrible excuse for not wanting to be here at orientation.*

I walked back out the orchestra building's front door just as Dad was getting to it.

I froze. "Uh . . . wrong day," I said.

"What?"

"It's the wrong day. No one's in there, Papi. Let's go home."

He looked around at all the cars in the lot and a kid walking into the building carrying something suspiciously resembling a cello case. "What's wrong?" Dad asked.

"I just wanna go home."

"Then let's go home."

On that quick drive home that felt like it took forever, I explained to Dad that I *knew* this was irresponsible, but I needed to move to a bigger city where I could take the chances I'd always wanted to take.

I fully expected him to talk me out of my wild ideas (that we couldn't afford) and into going to the easier school, the one to which I was already accepted, where I'd be living in a dorm with a roommate. The one where I would be getting scholarship money even though I *barely* graduated from high school, the same high school I was lucky to have had the chance to go to in the first place, one that I shouldn't have gotten into, though Dad had found a way anyway. I assumed he'd tell me that living closer to home just made obvious sense, that this dream just wasn't worth the risk.

He didn't.

Dad reminded me of the risks he and Mom took to get to America from Cuba: "We knew the risks were high. We knew we could die even just trying to do this. But we knew if we got to America, our children would be free to be whatever they wanted to be. To believe as they please. And to be driven by passion for what they were meant to accomplish and who they were meant to be. We wanted you to be able to choose what you wanted for your life. We didn't do it so you could settle."

That's all I needed to hear. I was off to Nashville the next week.

The only school in town that seemed open to the idea of admitting a new student the same day as freshmen were moving in was Trevecca Nazarene University. I had never even heard of it. When we arrived at the university, I'd packed only an overnight bag, because surely even if I got into this school, I'd have to wait till next semester. Dad made a beeline for the administration office, and within a few hours it was clear I wouldn't be making the nine-hour drive back to Jacksonville with him.

My dad is my hero. Risk. Expectation. Hope. Boy did he know that recipe long before I did.

So there we were, the very same day we arrived in Nashville, Dad clearly understanding that I was there to jump off a cliff. "Jump and the net will appear" I've heard (in a very intense acting-for-commercials course I took once). I was willing to find that out firsthand. And, Dad, he was all in.

With a single tear falling down his face, he looked at me. I could see he was holding in his heart all the hopes I had for myself, which were minuscule in comparison to the hopes he had already been holding for me long before I was even born. He left me with these parting words: "Don't come home till your dreams come true."

Dad got in the car and drove away. He called me about ninety seconds later to explain: "You know, you can always [*sniffle*] come home, right? I meant, don't give up. Never settle. Don't give in [*sniffle*]. There are great things ahead for you, son. I've always known that. And I've always known you're brave enough to go get them."

Abner

WE NEVER—AND I MEAN *NEVER*—
tell the true origin story for the name
JOHNNYSWIM. We've been known to
improvise fantastical tales during inter-
views, but they are always lies (and they
are never to be told twice).

But you know what? We're writing
a book. A freaking book. A full-fledged,
Convergent/Random-House-real-life-
publishing-company-with-due-dates-
and-editors-and-all-that *book. And it's by
us and about us!* (Sorry, I still think it's
crazy that I'm gonna one day be reading
these very words on the printed page,
shaking my head like, "What in the H-E-
double-hockey-sticks was I thinking writing this paragraph?!") If we were gonna
tell the truth anywhere, it would be here.
On our terms. So here goes. The 100
percent absolutely *true* story of where the
name JOHNNYSWIM came from. And,
honestly, the truth is a pretty wild story. It
may even sound just as crazy as the fake
ones. So here goes.

THE STORY OF JUANELO HIDALGO GOMEZ

There we were in the jungle.

It was getting dark faster than I would have expected, but the sun seemed to follow a different set of rules here below the equator. A mosquito the size of a small butterfly landed on my neck, and I swear I could hear it taking full gulps of my blood. When that hand smacked my collarbone, it hit so hard I was unable to tell which crunch was the mutant bug and which crunch was my neck. I came out of my daze furious and ready to swing and swear at whatever or whoever was certainly trying to ruin our secretive escape through the South American shrub. I turned with a lungful of air pressed against my lips and a fist pulled back, ready to whisper my shout as I flung a blow. I froze at the sight of the guilty one. Of course. Even with blood on her hand, a sunburned face covered with mud, and torn clothes, she still managed to look beautiful. *How!?* Amanda grinned a crooked smile while motioning to me with one hand to stay quiet and wiping off the remains of the demon spawn from her hand onto my shirt.

We've always been the ones to say yes before the question is even asked, but this time our decision had been a little crazy. At the time, there was an uprising against the government in Venezuela, with soldiers firing rubber bullets and tear gas into neighborhoods and schools (a war crime). In the weeks following the worst of it, a pastor friend of ours (we'll call him Pastor Felix) invited us to come down and visit some rural villages in need of a "pick me up." He'd preach the good news and we'd come along and sing some songs (at least one but often all three of the songs we knew in Spanish). Our presence was not a welcome one to the government or local militia.

Things got hairy at the second-to-last church we visited.

The churches we had gone to were all situated pretty close together. Hiking for a few hours or riding a boat up the Rio Orinoco for a couple of hours, we'd find another place of worship and try to cheer folks up. This time, we could hear the army (or militia; we didn't care to find out) coming into the village around song number two. When that song was over, Pastor Felix said some early farewells, the parishioners headed back to their homes, and Amanda and I set off on foot to get to the last church, four hours away. At the final location, a boat would take us out of the military red zone. But the army were still behind us. We had to forgo the last church visit and head directly to our emergency escape route.

Juanelo Hidalgo Gomez (Johnny, for short) was our guide through the jungle as we made our journey to the escape boat. A master fisherman, hunter, surviv-

alist, and translator, he wore a lot of hats for us on this trip. Some laughs are infectious, but Juanelo's was a CDC-certified, pandemic sort of infectious. His laughs could always penetrate the strongest mask. We couldn't have done any of the wild things we did without him, and we certainly wouldn't have done them with so much joy, either.

We knew the boat was waiting on the wrong side of the river from the direction we were traveling, but Juanelo said he had it handled. As we arrived at a wide stretch of river and saw the boat in the distance, we were *gassed*. All of us were sucking wind. Just as we began passing the water canteen around, Juanelo jumped into the river to swim to the other side to recover our rescue boat. The river held a variety of ways to die, from unmapped currents to wild predators—to name just some of the more popular ways to go out on the Rio Orinoco. Added to all that, we were there in the rainy season, so just as Juanelo reached the halfway mark in the river, the skies let loose. The cool rain on the hot river began to create a fog that was almost impenetrable.

We waited in a silence that was broken only by our ragged and increasingly worried-sounding breaths. Just then our rescue boat cracked through the fog, heading straight for us. Our relief bubbled into laughter, until we all noticed the obvious . . . there was no pilot at the helm of the boat.

The man whom all the gringos called Johnny had stared fear directly in the eye, as he often had, when he took his last swim to send the boat back to us and saved all of our lives.

We will never know exactly what took Juanelo but, though he is gone, I can still hear his laugh. Amanda and I will never forget him. We wanted his name to live on in legacy in any way we could make happen. So for us, the mantra "Swim, Johnny, swim" means to put others first at all costs, fearlessly and with joy. To us, it means service is greater than self. It's something "Johnny" gave his life teaching us.

We are forever grateful.

And *that* is the real meaning behind the name JOHNNYSWIM.

Amanda

LET ME TELL YOU SOMETHING about Abner. His flair for drama is unmatched. Levels 0 to 10 on the scale are for amateurs. When Abner's kicks in, it kicks in at an 11. Take, for example, our first Valentine's Day. It started off like most other couples' Valentine's evening: some flowers, a nice dinner, maybe there was a card or little gift. I was honestly just excited to dress up and have a nice meal. But lo, Abner had more in store. The sweet start to the date was absolutely forgettable compared to the end, where I found myself enjoying a picnic in the living room of his tiny apartment, surrounded by candles, wine, cheese (he could have won me with cheese alone), and a live string trio playing old Gershwin love songs. Yep, you read that right. My handsome busboy managed to figure out a way to hire a live string trio to play in his apartment. When Abner aims to show his love, he shows it in bold capital letters, italicized, and filling the page.

That's why three years or so later, as our relationship galloped toward a proposal, I expected something amazing. Our time together was what every good love story should be: full of fighting and tension, making up and enough making out to keep it interesting but still relatively holy. Our families melded. His nieces and nephews slowly became my own, and vice versa. Our parents became friends. Our traditions overlapped and dissolved into each other. Our stories weaved themselves together bit by bit, day by day, memory by memory. We knew we were meant to be together. There was no question. I could feel the proposal coming. Marriage was just a matter of time at that point. Time . . . and money.

Unfortunately, despite playing lots of four-hour shows for very few people at Asian fusion restaurants, we weren't billionaires yet. Where was our money tree? It was time. Our star skipped and stumbled along instead of shooting, which was fine with me. But the very small sliver of myself that is Type A wondered how we would pay the bills and make a life on a part-time barista, part-time musician income. The ability to jointly afford exactly one fajita platter to share at a crappy Mexican restaurant does not a life make. So I tried convincing Abner and myself that I didn't need a ring or a proposal. I was fine waiting until we more ready and responsible.

Neither of us believed me.

Abner

I STARTED SAVING FOR THE WED-ding from the first day we started dating. That's right—I started putting money away for a ring even before our first kiss. Why? Probably because I'm a psycho. I knew what style of ring Amanda wanted, so I visited a jewelry store where my friend had bought the engagement ring for his Mrs. I picked one out, then proceeded to visit it once a week for months. I was making friends with the ring. And the store owners as well.

There was no way I could actually buy the ring. I had no credit, and I couldn't get credit from the store. My parents didn't have enough money to loan me. All I could afford to give the jewelry store was a 10-percent down payment. It didn't matter. I kept visiting that ring.

I had a plan. Two years from the time I started picking out a ring, and three years to the day we first kissed, I would propose to Amanda in Paris, on October 1, 2008.

Amanda

AUGUST OF 2008 ROLLED AROUND and carried my twenty-fifth birthday with it (don't do the math in your head. I'm forever twenty-five). My friends whispered guesses as to when Abner would propose, feeling the inevitability looming. All I could think about was Abner having just asked me for grocery money the week before. I failed to mention this little fact to my friends because I'm a believer in keeping hope alive for everyone. Maybe he was saving up for a ring and thus couldn't afford bread and eggs. How was I to know?! What I did know was that he was being sneakier than normal. He'd rush to close his laptop when I walked by or suddenly change the subject on a phone call as soon as I entered the room. This was very unusual. I got excited and played dumb.

Sure enough, I was wrong. My birthday came and went. Nothing happened. No ring. No proposal. Just same-old same-old with a side of, "Can I borrow twenty dollars?" Regardless, my mother and I casually began planning a spring "elopement" on a visit to their beach house in Florida, a little wedding for just our closest people. The house was small and intimate, snugly nestled on a dirt road with the bay on one side and the gulf on the other. I had always wanted an au-

tumn wedding in a small, candlelit chapel, but a beach wedding during spring break could work too, right?

I ignored my naked ring finger as my mom and I made deposits on everything from dresses to florists. My dad, on the other hand, mocked me about the bad luck of planning a wedding before a proposal. I knew I was being a little extra desperate, but dang, Dad.

Chill! We're broke and figuring it out, okay?

I hoped he knew something I didn't.

Either way, I was slowly growing used to the idea of a nonproposal proposal. The anticipation for an elaborate engagement spawned by Abner's sneakiness had vanished, but it didn't matter. My eyes were set on the marriage prize, which was surely coming with or without a fancy ring.

The day after we got back from our trip to Florida, I woke up to a very nervous Abner. I lived at my parents' house at the time, which was pretty far from civilization, so I was shocked to see him at 7:00 A.M.

"Has something terrible happened? No? Then why are you here and where is my coffee?" As I've previously mentioned, I am in no way, shape, or form a morning person. Getting out of bed and to the door felt like a gut punch, and the lack of

caffeine in Abner's hand felt like hatred. I thought he knew me.

We made our way to the kitchen, Abner still nervous and me still half-asleep. But then I noticed something. He held a card in a green envelope with illegible writing on it. "I need to tell you I had to change our dinner plans for our anniversary," Abner said.

My eyes, still burning, tried to focus on his face and pick up any spare clues as to what the heck he was talking about and why the heck I was awake. For one, our anniversary was two days away. Who cares at 7:00 A.M. where we're going to dinner in two days? For two, the plans he was changing consisted of a full day of eating at restaurants we loved around town. Breakfast at Waffle House, followed by coffee at Fido, followed by lunch at P.F. Chang's for old times' sake, and a pasta dinner. It was my kind of celebration, but not one that required a lot of planning.

Abner picked up on my confusion and slowly pushed the green envelope toward me. "I know we had planned on Italian for dinner, but we're going to a French restaurant instead."

Still tired and dumb and caffeineless, I shrugged and asked where the French restaurant was located in Nashville. I'd never heard of one.

"Oh, it's in St. Germain," he said.

He's confused.
"You mean Germantown?"
The envelope slid closer to me. "Nope. I mean St. Germain."
That's in Paris.
Suddenly I was wide awake! I ripped open the envelope, now very aware of the potential it held. The puzzle pieces formed a picture I could finally make out. Sure enough, tucked into that little green envelope were two first-class tickets to Paris for the next morning. FIRST CLASS TO PARIS! In just twenty-four hours, we'd be in the air heading to ten days in my favorite city. I jumped off the stool in excitement, and in one forceful jerk, threw my neck out. I couldn't turn it in either direction. It was locked and tight. But it didn't matter. Nothing could stop my celebration. Nothing except one thought: "You're *going to propose*!" I squealed.

Without missing a beat, Abner stopped me. This wasn't an engagement trip, he wanted me to know right away. He didn't want expectations to kill the beauty of the thing at hand: a trip he had planned for months before talk of a wedding existed.

He had a point.

I got my nails done later that day just in case, though, with Abner's sister Abdi. (I also may have looked ever so gingerly through his bag for a ring like a crazy person. Don't tell.)

Abner

FIRST OFF, I *DID* BRING AMANDA coffee when I surprised her that morning with the card and the trip to Paris. I had everything planned out, including something very important. I remember something she told me when we first started dating: "I know this is early, but if we ever get married, don't let me be that girl who has nasty-looking nails when she gets engaged."

This is why I asked my sister Abdi to take Amanda to get her nails done before we left. I still needed to get the ring, so I went to the jeweler I'd been visiting for months to try to secure the deal. At the time, I was working at P.F. Chang's as a busser, someone who clears tables and brings the food out for patrons. I hadn't quite made it to the status of being a server. So needless to say, I didn't exactly have the money I needed to pay for the ring.

When I got to the ring store, I told them the truth: "Look, here's the deal. I don't have the money for this ring yet. I don't have the credit. I just need you to let me take it. We're going to Paris tomorrow. I just surprised her and gave her the tickets. We're going first-class. I spent all my money on those tickets, so I don't have enough money to pay for this ring."

I gave them my license and my moth-er's address, then told them I planned on paying this back as soon as I could: "I'll pay it off more quickly than if I had store credit. I'm going to pay this down as soon as possible. I just need to take this ring to Paris."

They were kind enough to say yes.

On the plane, Amanda was still convinced that I had concocted some big plan. "Oh, you're not taking me to Paris and *not* proposing," she said. "I know you've got the ring."

"Babe, I ran out of money. I spent all my money on this. We know we want to get married. This is our engagement trip. I gave you an engagement trip and a memory instead of a ring."

I wasn't lying. I was out of money, and I had spent all of it on this trip.

"Go ahead and look through my bag," I dared her.

If she had looked through my stuff, she would have found the ring in my sock. It was *so conspicuous.* Thankfully, she believed me.

"I was thinking we could go to the famous Parisian flea market and find a ring there," I said.

Okay, so this might have been stretching the truth a bit.

Amanda thought it was a beautiful idea.

Amanda

WE LANDED THE MORNING OF our anniversary: October 1, 2008. It was rainy and chilly and perfectly romantic. We strolled the streets like zombies in a fog of jet lag, feeling high off the beauty of the city. Abner scheduled the day for us, and even though this was very unlike him, it didn't set off any alarms. As we walked the Left Bank of the Seine, he apologized sheepishly for not being able to afford a ring once he had planned this trip. I liked his suggestion of going to the flea market and finding a cheap ring instead. He had budgeted enough for one really nice meal, and then baguettes and butter would have to sustain us the rest of the time, but if we did that, he promised he would have enough left over for something little. What could be more romantic than a beautiful little flea market ring? I could get down! We'd pass it on to one of our kids, and then one day our grandkids would fight over it. It would carry its own sentimental inheritance for generations. The subject changed, and Abner kept talking, but all I could think about was the cute little story we'd tell our kids one day.

The "one nice meal" was that first night. Lapérouse used to house one of the king's wine cellars, or something like that, but now it was known as one of the top romantic restaurants in the city. Everything about it screamed fancy and French, including the maître d'. He seemed confused about our reservation. Or upset. Or both. I'm not sure, but he pulled Abner aside and whisper-screamed in a French accent before seating us in the dining room, where we were soon enjoying the fanciest meal we had ever had to date. I couldn't tell you one thing we ate because I couldn't read the menu and didn't even want to. It was delicious and decadent in a way only French food can be. My happy place had been found. Abner seemed distracted by the minor kerfuffle with the host, but honestly, thanks to all the glorious butter and flavor I was consuming, I really didn't care.

Abner

I HAD THE WHOLE DAY PLANNED out for our three-year anniversary: where we'd have breakfast, when we'd nap, which museum we'd go to, what we'd have for lunch . . . everything. I planned on proposing in a private room in this famous restaurant called Lapérouse. It was initially built as a three-story private mansion; King Louis XVI's personal beverage maker founded it in 1766 and turned it into a wine market.

The day was perfect until we arrived at the restaurant. For starters, we didn't get the private room my friend had reserved for us. Then I learned about the history of the romantic establishment. Lapérouse became famous for men taking their mistresses there. They would go to one of those private rooms and pay with diamonds for the services of a lady. The lady would sit in front of the mirror, and they'd scratch it with the diamond to prove its integrity.

This is where you take hookers!?

Suddenly I realized I couldn't propose in this place. The vibe was all wrong. We didn't have a private room. Plus—Amanda wasn't my mistress! But this had been my plan all along. I didn't have a Plan B.

I did know, however, that I had made a promise to myself: *I'm never proposing* *at the Eiffel Tower.* This was my number one rule for proposing to Amanda in Paris: No Eiffel Tower. I thought it was too cheesy. It's a radio tower that somehow came to signify love in the city of lights. To me, it was just bad marketing, and nothing more.

It's genius marketing, actually.

It just didn't make sense to me—the radio tower, all of it. Nope. I wasn't proposing there.

Now that the restaurant was a bust, I quickly got us out of there and found a cab. I had to propose before midnight.

"Where to?" the driver asked.

"The Eiffel Tower."

Amanda

DINNER ENDED, AND ABNER seemed to be taking a hit from the old jet lag bat. I had taken a nap, but he, not wanting to miss a single moment, had walked the city instead. Now he was hurting. We left the restaurant, ready to wander some more, but Abner seemed agitated. There were too many people everywhere, and he was over it. He'd always made fun of people's fascination with the Eiffel Tower, but before I knew it, he had hailed a cab, and we were heading that way. Unlike him, I was thrilled. I'm a sucker for landmarks.

The cab pulled up just as the tower was in full sparkle mode. I had seen it do this before on other trips, but catching this moment at the top of every hour still to this day feels like a little beautiful miracle. Unfortunately, Abner once again was not happy with the situation. He didn't like where we were standing, so instead of taking the spectacle in, he was pulling me by the arm and we were running to the other side of the tower. He didn't even seem to hear me whining, "Why are we ruuuuuuuunning?" He just dragged me under the tower, away from the street and onto the lawn. Somehow even being pulled to a run felt romantic in the moment, which is good because otherwise I probably would have been annoyed. After a short sprint, we arrived at a spot he deemed acceptable for viewing the sparkles just in time for . . . wait for it . . . a small French poodle to take a crap right in front of us.

Abner

11:00 P.M. WHEN WE ARRIVED AT the Eiffel Tower and stood there as it sparkled, I knew I didn't want to propose beneath it. So I rushed us over to the first part of the lawn, where I could position her just right so she could see the whole thing glistening while I got down on one knee.

11:03 P.M. If I was gonna get this done while the Eiffel Tower was still sparkling, I only had two minutes left. All I needed was the guy walking his little French poodle to pass us by so I could give the speech I'd memorized and rehearsed in front of a mirror. But the guy stopped so this little dog could take the biggest dump I've ever seen.

11:05 P.M. The magnificent glow of the Eiffel Tower shut off. As the guy walked off with the poodle, I stood there staring at the crap he hadn't bothered to pick up. This poop symbolized what this proposal had become. Everything had been working out today except for the crowning piece. I just couldn't believe what I was looking at.

Did he really just leave that? This is too perfect and too horrible.

For a moment I contemplated my life while staring at dog poop. Then I realized I had fifty-five minutes before the tower would light up again.

I give up.

Amanda

YOU WOULD HAVE THOUGHT
Abner had lost all his money in a high-stakes bet. He was not happy. The night was too beautiful to be bummed about some dog poop, though, and there was a gorgeous over-the-top bridge I had seen earlier in the day that I had been wanting to walk across. I suggested once again that we visit the bridge and watch the tower light up again in an hour. A twinkle returned to his eye, and the dog poop was forgotten.

Abner

SHE HAD BEEN WANTING TO GO
to this bridge all day. She thought it looked so beautiful, but I told her we didn't have time. I'm not really a planner, but when I make a plan, I'm obsessed.

As we approached the bridge, Amanda started to hug me, but I had the ring in my jacket pocket, so I had to think fast so she wouldn't feel it. I quickly maneuvered away from her with a fancy dance, just to get to her other side. She wondered what I was doing. I just told her I was caught up in the romance of the moment. I thought I looked smooth. Meanwhile, I just looked like a drunk's apprentice.

When we finally reached the bridge, it was incredible. It rests over the Seine with a perfect view of the Eiffel Tower on one side and a view of Notre-Dame on the other.

Oh man, this is too perfect. It's gonna happen.

Amanda

PONT ALEXANDRE III IS MORE beautiful in person than it is in pictures. It's covered in gold accents, and an angel carrying a torch graces its center. It's worn and weathered in a way that gives it more life instead of less. It's gaudy but honest. I gasped as we drew close, and our hurried skip slowed to a patient step as we took in all the intricacies of her beauty and let her drench the moment in awe.

I don't remember the details of what happened next. It was all a blur, but somehow, some way, Abner took a knee next to that glorious angel. His quivering hand held a ring box, but I didn't even see what it carried. I dropped to my knees and embraced him, my neck still stiff from the excitement of a few days earlier. Somewhere in there he asked if I would marry him, and apparently through tears and gasping I said yes. He put the ring on my finger. Suddenly I knew where all his grocery money had gone.

Abner

I HAD THIS WHOLE SPEECH WRIT- ten. Yet right when I got down on my knee, I was so nervous and shook up that I couldn't remember any of it. Not a word.

There's this thing that happens in shows when you forget the words to the song, but you just keep going. You keep singing. If you don't overthink and just open your mouth, 99 percent of the time you'll sing the right words. So I decided to use this same strategy. I'd just keep speaking, and the words would come back to me.

"Babe, I love you. I *love* you. Oh, do I love you. Like, really, truly love you."

The words definitely weren't coming back to me.

For a moment, she thought my jet lag was speaking again. For a brief moment, I remembered one other thing she had always wanted during a proposal. Her nails were done, but she also wanted a photographer to be there at this very moment.

"Sorry there's not a photographer," I quickly said. Then asked, "Will you marry me?"

The least romantic proposal of all time.

"Are you serious??" Amanda said, falling to her knees and giving me a big hug and kiss.

As we held each other, I encouraged her to put on the ring, this ring I didn't own yet. I pictured it falling into the Seine and ruining this night. But nothing could do that.

Later that night we started a tradition that continues to this day: We celebrated with champagne and french fries.

Amanda

A WHOLE HOUR WENT BY. WE called our families while still sitting in the middle of the bridge next to our angel. Of course, they had already been told about Abner's grand plan, which is why my dad had been reveling in teasing me about our wedding. Before we knew it, the tower was sparkling again for the last time that night, and so was my finger.

To this day, I still don't know how he pulled it off. Part of me hopes to never find out. Remind me not to read what he writes in this chapter, lest the mystery be gone. I don't want any of those mundane details. He told me everything I needed to know that night, in bold capital letters, italicized, and filling the page.

Amanda

OUR WEDDING IS SMALL AND wonderful. My mother transforms their little house at the end of the key, the one between the bay and the gulf, into a Moroccan-inspired retreat, with a hint of Ibiza nightclub. I ask her for only candles everywhere. I want moody. I want holy. I want vibey. I want monastery romance. She says, "Sure, honey, but let's add some multicolored strobe lights and neon orbs." Apparently, she wants just a little bit of club added to the mix.

I don't care enough to argue. I am the last of her daughters to get married, and I want her to revel in the whole process. I want her to feel like it is her celebration, too, because it is. The night will be both of our parents' entrance-into-empty-nestdom party. They deserve to dance, and they definitely deserve a drink. So, in hopes of keeping wedding drama to a minimum, I give her five things I really care about: the guest list, the dress, the food, the photographer, and the music. Everything else is fair game. I have my groom, my people, and large platters of food being passed around at family-style tables. I am happy. The rest is just minutia.

Sure, there are moments when I question this game plan. Let's just say there is a lot of pink and orange when I asked for blush and coral. But as my mom stands on her balcony overlooking the party at the end of the night, she dances, holds her friends, and smiles with her big ol' beautiful smile, shining like one of those dang Ibiza strobe lights. It is amazing.

We don't know at this moment how little time we have left with her. What a gift of a memory, worth every bit of too many wrong colors and neon lighting.

The wedding starts with another gift of a memory. Omar, the quintessential storyteller, tells a classic story about Abner being in love at age seven (see page 38). We don't know then how little time we have remaining with Omar, either, but if it's possible to steal the show at a wedding, he does it. Unanimously, everyone's favorite part of the wedding is Omar's speech. Eleven years later, I still think it's mine, too, other than the marrying Abner part.

Like the dumb babies we are, Abner and I cry for the majority of the ceremony. When I say Abner and I cry during the whole ceremony, I mean we full-on, snot-flowing, ugly cry. We lose all ability to control our emotions. Not great for pictures, to be honest, but the moment feels weightier than we expected. The holiness catches us off guard, and thus I cry off all my self-done makeup, as you do when Heaven comes close. The whole day is like that—sacred surprises around every corner.

Massive tufts of clouds shelter our eyes and skin from the sun, and to my knowledge not a soul gets sunburned. That right there is a Florida spring break wedding miracle, just another sacred gift. We and our sixty-two or so guests dine on the beach at sunset and eat cake on the lawn and later enjoy mini burgers and fries at midnight. We drink too much wine, but still somehow have cases left over for years. And, yes, we dance like we are in an Ibiza nightclub. Our little sandy Florida wedding bears little resemblance to the wedding teenage Amanda wanted, but it is everything she deep down, really, truthfully wanted. Life and weddings be like that sometimes. Yes, I know that's bad grammar, but they do.

Abner and I leave the next morning on a too-early, almost-missed flight to Jamaica. The boutique hotel has only a few rooms, so it feels like our own palace, with peacocks roaming the walkways and butlers offering us a signature "mangosa" every time we walk out of our room. Unfortunately, I manage to get a mean case of strep throat the day before we leave. If you're trying to tone down the sex appeal on your honeymoon, just go ahead and get what your doctor will call the worst case of strep he's ever seen. That will do it. So Abner enjoys the bottle of rum from the all-inclusive minibar on the last day of our honeymoon while I drool on a towel-covered pillow, afraid to swallow, since my throat is full of razor blades. It's not pleasant, but luckily Abner is a great nurse and doesn't annul the marriage.

The problem bigger than the loss of my feminine mystique so quickly in the marriage is the fact that we have a few weeks' worth of booked shows to play as soon as we get home. Actually, our honeymoon is shorter than most, just a few days, so we can fly back to Nashville and hop in our dear friend Will Solomon's SUV for shows around the South. (Bless him for touring with newlyweds in a shared hotel room. Yikes! Please never sue us.) I self-medicate with enough ibuprofen to get through the first leg of our flight home, find an urgent care and pharmacy on our layover, and make it to Nashville feeling tired but already better with antibiotics in my bloodstream. We have one day to rest up, unpack, do laundry, open a few wedding gifts, and head out on the road. It is a wild schedule, but we are newlyweds just beginning to actually taste some dreams coming true, the first of which is our finally being married.

Turns out this sort of adventure is all the way on-brand for us. It's been eleven years. Tours haven't stopped, wild adventures haven't stopped, and I still don't think I've fully unpacked a bag.

THE MARTHA WASHINGTON INN

Abner

WHEN I SAY *NEVER*, I MEAN *NEVER*.

We never tell the truth about the origin of the band name JOHNNYSWIM.

But you know what? *We're writing a freaking book!* Here we are, in your living room or on your nightstand or collecting dust on your bookshelf or coffee table. In this very moment, we are an invited guest into the most honored room in your house. We are guests in your mind. We are a voice in your head. (I wonder what my voice sounds like in your head?) The privilege is certainly all ours. We wouldn't besmirch the occasion with a *lie*.

So, finally, *here* is the very true origin story of the name JOHNNYSWIM.

I'm never quick to say a place is haunted, but I guarantee you the Martha Washington Inn was. Mercy. We were in Abingdon, Virginia, playing at some I-don't-remember-what as the no-band-name singing duo "Amanda and Abner." The show wrapped, and we hung out with some friends for a long nightcap before checking in to lay our heads down at the hotel for a few hours. We had an all-too-early-morning flight the next day. The neo-zombie who checked us in exhibited the joy of a thumbtack along with the vocal range of exactly one note. After check-in, Amanda went to grab us breakfast menus, and I headed up to the room with *all* of the bags.

Just the thought of the Martha Washington Inn brings back the taste of dust in the air.

The first thing I really remember is the unique way the lights flickered, not all the way from off to on but just sort of phasing between dim shades of yellow and orange. The subtle obfuscation had me staring down the long white hallway, wondering if my mind was playing tricks on me. Carrying all of Amanda's bags used a decidedly large amount of physical and mental fortitude. I felt the strength of my muscles wane when the strap of Amanda's heaviest bag (her toiletry bag, somehow?) began to slip off my arm, and I surrendered my complete attention to the eerily empty, dusty hallway.

I got the strangest feeling.

You know it. You may even be feeling it right now: The urge to look over your left shoulder just slowly enough to hopefully ward off whatever may be looking back at you. The sense that you're being watched. The knowledge that you are consciously avoiding any reflective surface that might show you instantly what is behind you.

The fact was, I didn't want to see it. I could feel *something* there. It? Whom? I didn't want to know. I wanted to be alone and surrounded by people, all at the same time. It wasn't just the goose bumps going up my arms that disturbed me, either. I felt so sad all of a sudden, like I was dropped into a cold lake, and the water itself was a potion for loneliness.

I kept my eyes glued to the hallway's central chandelier, that sole source of light like a dying ember. I was staying alive by sheer force of will. I stared *hard* at the light. It was now my best and only friend in the universe as my feet grew ever more rooted into the thick green carpet beneath them. The silence grew louder as the air seemed to take life and pulse at its own pace within my lungs and ears. Colder. Sadder. Cold. Fear. Sadness. It was so cold. Just as the crescendo became unbearable, the silence too loud . . . darkness.

Pure darkness. The kind that you could measure on a scale.

Heavy.

I knew I was no longer alone.

I'd like to say I ran "like a man." But as Amanda recalls, "The shrieks of a preteen K-pop fan" announced my rush down the stairs (no one takes the elevator in an emergency). I tumbled down the last few steps and rolled up in a heap at Amanda's feet.

"Guess someone told you the old rumor?" she said.

"Huh?"

"Yeah, they say the original cook of this place was drowned in the pool by an angry mob. He supposedly walks the hallways at night."

Cold. Fear. Water.

She laughed at me, and said, "Swim, Johnny, swim!"

I shivered.

She rubbed it in. "Yeah, that's what they apparently said as they threw him in, but it's an old made-up tale to draw tourists. Let's go to bed."

To this day, Amanda still mocks me for being such a scaredy-cat, saying, "Swim, Johnny, swim." She went to such great lengths to make sure I wouldn't forget what a big sissy I was that night that "we" even decided to name the band after it.

And *that* is the true story of how the band name JOHNNYSWIM came to be.

A Conversation Between Abner & Amanda

AMANDA: When we first met, we started to build a community in Nashville before we were married.

ABNER: We'd have family dinner every Thursday night, and everybody would get together and cook. It's something we kind of do now, but we do it so much better now, foodwise.

AMANDA: Yeah, everybody'd bring something cheap from the grocery store and we'd all put it together. These family dinners were one of my favorite things, because I hadn't before really experienced community like I did when I first moved to Nashville. We weren't like, *Oh yeah, let's go to a club, let's go see a movie.* We actually did things where we were investing in our group, our community.

ABNER: It was such a communal event. Like, we'd get to the movie thirty minutes early, forty-five minutes early. Just because it was so much about the hang. It didn't matter if we were there an hour before the movie started.

AMANDA: Everything was always communal in those three years after we first started dating. Then when we got married, I feel like that got kind of lost. In our first year of marriage, we had friends and we would still hang out a lot. But I feel like we didn't have the same sense of community as before.

ABNER: It began to feel like we were spinning our wheels in Nashville, like people didn't know what to do with us— two brown folks singing a kind-of folk, kind-of R&B, kind-of pop music. What I remember most are the meetings—all those meetings. God bless them. People trying to help us, but nobody knew what to do. And I remember leaving one, one of the last ones, thinking, *If we have one more meeting—*

AMANDA: I think I'm done with meetings.

ABNER: Yeah. What was it even like? I remember being so excited. But why? There was this one music executive who was friendly. He'd sit with us and he'd give us advice, because it wasn't like we were listening to music. What were we doing in those meetings?

AMANDA: They were kind of like, "So, where do you guys see yourself? What do you guys feel like you might need?" It was always like somebody was trying to figure out if there was a way they could latch on to us without actually latching

on. Like, maybe they could help a little bit, and then if we happened to do well, they wanted to be there to hitch on. But honestly, to be fair, we didn't know what we were doing.

ABNER: Yeah.

AMANDA: We were still discovering our sound. We were playing a bunch of random shows. I think at that point we were still waiting for somebody to bring us to the next level.

ABNER: The common mistake an artist makes is that you always think you're dependent on somebody else: *Well, I would do my own thing if only I got discovered by the right person . . . We've got a great song . . . but . . .* There are obviously varying shades of gray in each person, right? It's easy to believe you're just waiting on someone or something else to propel you where you're meant to be. There's the imaginary artist who hasn't yet made a career for himself or herself—

AMANDA: The theoretical.

ABNER: The theoretical artist. Either (a), they believe *I've done everything I can. It's just that, you know, people need to start paying attention.* Or (b), they think, *I'm just not connected enough.*

AMANDA: Right.

ABNER: Maybe they're right. Sure. But even in the most connected cities, and with the most connected people, it's *always* about the work the artist puts into it. So, at the time, we were artists waiting to be discovered. We were waiting for somebody, some eagle, to swoop in and take us to that higher echelon. That way their prowess would become ours. "Well, you know who discovered JOHNNYSWIM, right?"

AMANDA: That's what I grew up with. Who discovered whom—

ABNER: Elton John was discovered at the Troubadour. So-and-so's first concert was at the Roxy.

AMANDA: Right.

ABNER: You spend years thinking the secret to success is *that moment of discovery. When it's really the years of obscurity that define you.*

AMANDA: I think, maybe, back in the day, record labels played a different role. You know, especially before there was social media and before we could stream music or whatever else. But I think we also had an added handicap, because I think most people thought, "Oh, you come from a family of musicians. So surely you just have all the right connections."

ABNER: Right.

AMANDA: "And you can just walk in any door." And, yeah, we probably could have gone through a bunch of doors and had somebody offer, "Yeah, we'll just put you under our wing." But we were very anti-that.

ABNER: At the time it was like asking a dinosaur to give you advice on fossil fuels.

AMANDA: Right.

ABNER: The current music industry is built off the death of the old one. We were beginning right at that change.

AMANDA: Right at that change. It's like they didn't know what they were doing. We might not know what we're doing, but they actually really *still* don't know what they're doing. But they're stuck in some old way. And now people wanted to add on, "She's Donna Summer's daughter." And so I felt like we were fighting against a lot of that, too.

ABNER: One hundred percent.

AMANDA: We wanted to be able to have somebody discover us and help us. But we didn't want somebody to use my mom to do that.

ABNER: We knew we needed to get out of Nashville. Honestly, my move from Jacksonville to Nashville did make a dif-

ference. I was now around people playing music all the time. Brian Elmquist from the wonderful band The Lone Bellows. The Lone Bellow—

AMANDA: Don't add that extra *s*.

ABNER: Why? Donna Summers.

AMANDA: *[Laughs.]*

ABNER: Lone Bellows.

AMANDA: I have a problem with those extra *s*'s.

ABNER: Krogers.

AMANDA: Exactly.

ABNER: Triggered! It was fascinating for me to go from Jacksonville to Nashville. Suddenly I was surrounded by people who were pursuing something, and I felt like there was traction.

AMANDA: Yeah.

ABNER: But we got to the point where we felt like we were spinning our wheels, and we were swimming upstream a little bit. Nashville—the DNA of Nashville music—wasn't fitting what we saw ourselves doing. So, the answer for us was going to be L.A. or New York. Because we were looking for an apartment in New York. At the same time, we were looking for a place in L.A. But what's this about L.A.?

AMANDA: I hated L.A. I lived in L.A. once and I hated it. If there's one thing I knew, it's that I was never gonna move to L.A. I was actually born here in L.A., and I still was like, *I'll never go back. I will not go back.* New York was the place I was always trying to get back to. I loved being there. But I was kind of spinning my wheels there. It was so fun to be able to do modeling stuff and meet all these people and have this independent awakening on my own. But then I went to Nashville and discovered people who loved what they did. That was kind of a whole other thing. I just kept thinking that now that Abner and I were married and we were doing our own thing, New York would be such a fun place to go. But I just kept getting this sense that we were going to be in L.A. I even wrote it in my journal: *What is this about L.A.?* in the middle of blabbering, diary styling: *"Dear Diary, I went to the store and I don't know what to do."* And then it was just like, *What is this about L.A.?* Because I felt that.

ABNER: That's so cool.

AMANDA: And I remember calling you and being like—

ABNER: Oh, that's right!

AMANDA: "I know you're not going to like this. You're not going to like this. But

I keep feeling like we're supposed to move to L.A." And you were like, "Dang it! I totally feel the same way. I didn't want to say anything to you about it because I feel the same way." And we were like, *Crap . . .*

ABNER: Right. 'Cause my experience of L.A. was all just douchey people and everyone trying too hard or shaking your hand—the classic L.A. move of shaking your hand while looking over your shoulder. Unless you're the famous person, the big dog in the room.

AMANDA: Nobody is actually looking each other in the eye. It almost seems like it's the anti-community place. And I feel like for a lot of people, it almost is. For many, there's no community here and everybody's transient. Everybody's trying for something. So, you totally miss out on connecting with other people. And I remember even your mom being like, "What about your marriage?"

ABNER: Literally. When I called my mom—I know you remember this, but I'm telling it anyway. When I called my mom to say, "We're moving to L.A.," she started crying and said, "What about your marriage?" I was so confused. "Mom. The worst thing that could happen to our marriage was if we moved to Jacksonville."

AMANDA: *[Laughs.]*

ABNER: That'd be the worst.

AMANDA: Or just stayed in Nashville. We were in quicksand.

ABNER: Ooh.

AMANDA: But we came out here. And the surprise of all surprises, once we got settled, was that, oh, look, there's a bunch of other people who feel the same way we feel. They aren't just here because they want to do something cool. They actually feel like they're supposed to be here. *I don't have people, but I'm here. I'm trying to be obedient to what I feel like I'm being called to do. And so I'm out here and I kind of feel like I'm just floating around.* And we all found each other in the same waters.

ABNER: Wow.

AMANDA: We built a life in a life raft that we all jumped into together and had the best time.

ABNER: Yeah, absolutely. People who are still our closest friends today.

AMANDA: I feel like you remember this. You were driving near the airport because we were about to drop off a friend. And he said, "I feel like this next season for you . . ."

ABNER: I hate this part.

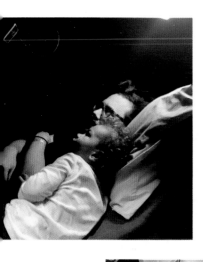

AMANDA: Remember what he said?

ABNER: Pastor Dan Fessler from New Jersey. I was waiting for the word because we'd left Nashville and come to L.A. to really get traction. This is where it was going to happen. We were gonna build a fan base—all things that ended up happening—but not in our timeline and not in our way. Not the way we imagined them. We were in L.A., so I expected somebody like a Pastor Dan, somebody who's been in our life for a long time, to say, "This is it. This is the moment. You took the risk. Here comes the reward."

AMANDA: Yeah. And he was like, "Actually—"

ABNER: "This season is going to be a contentment season." And I did not want to hear "contentment." What I wanted to hear was "Work!" Because we didn't have kids yet. *"Work your tail off! You're gonna work so hard and there's going to be so much reward!"* Risk. Work. Reward. I'm not trying to just risk and reward. I know there's work. We both did. We were happy to work three hundred days a year, which we ended up doing. We were happy to absolutely commit our lives to a thing and continually risk and have hope for these things. The *last* thing I wanted to hear from a mentor like Pastor Dan—someone who felt like he had his

finger on the pulse of our lives and our trajectory—was that the coming season was gonna be one of contentment. To me, contentment is an eighty-year-old man sitting in a rocking chair on his front porch remembering the good old days. Not two hungry twentysomethings who just risked everything to move to a city three thousand miles away with no money in their pockets. That didn't seem like it was gonna be the banner for those coming years of moving to L.A.

AMANDA: Right.

ABNER: I am so grateful that the banner that hung over those first few years in L.A. was *contentment,* because contentment ended up meaning finding your people. Contentment meant finding your purpose and finding out who you are. We wouldn't have a career today if we didn't have that season of contentment. What's Paul say in the Bible? I'm paraphrasing here: "I know how to live with little and how to live when I have much, and I've been happy in both." I always assumed real happiness would come when we got the career we wanted. 'Cause that's even part of knowing your purpose, right? *Because that's what I'm supposed to do. Once I get there, I'll be really happy.* No! We had to learn how to be happy, broke. Honestly. It's maybe the happiest we've ever been. Then there was our best friend, Darren Lau. A hero of the ages. The absolute best friend a man can have.

AMANDA: When we didn't have enough money to pay our light bills . . .

ABNER: Our lights got cut off while we were hanging out one afternoon.

AMANDA: And he went and paid it for us.

ABNER: He grabbed the electric bill, ran out, drove away, and paid our electric bill for us while we were pooling our money together. We were saving quarters to be able to buy bottles of wine. And we'd buy Two-Buck Chuck.

AMANDA: And that leads me to another great thing. We would have people over just like we did in Nashville when we first met. We'd have these family dinners, and every Thursday night we would get together. But we were so broke that we would have to scrape together quarters. And I remember it was thirty-five dollars—that was my budget for Thursday nights to be able to buy groceries to feed us and our twelve friends.

ABNER: Whoo.

AMANDA: Everybody brought something. But I'd always want to make sure that we had the main dish, and if we needed wine or drinks or whatever. A lot of times we'd do a theme night, so I wanted to make sure we had enough money to decorate a little or buy some flowers for that night, to make it special. I remember, actually, it was thirty dollars and then we bumped it up to thirty-five dollars, and it was like—

ABNER: That was a faith move.

AMANDA: That was a faith move. And sometimes the rest came out of quarters.

ABNER: You remember Shane Stevens gave us a hundred-dollar gift card to Trader Joe's, and we wept?

AMANDA: We cried because we were like, *This is going to last us forever!*

ABNER: Probably did.

AMANDA: It wasn't just a bummer when Pastor Dan said that to us about contentment. I remember driving home in silence for a while after our talk with him. It felt like we were mourning, because we had just risked so much to be here. We were stepping out in faith, and we didn't have a bunch of money, and we didn't know how it was going to work, but we believed that it was going to work. We were ready to risk it. Then for him to say, "Oh, you're going to be content" to us meant that it was going to be a slow honeymoon time.

Really? No. This was supposed to be a season of work. His words made it feel like we had to let go of this dream that we had, this image that we had of what our life was going to be like when we moved out to L.A. I still pull from that season even now, because when things get busy, things get crazy, it's easy to lose that sense of contentment. It's super easy. I feel like it's more easy now to be negative than it was before. Back then we had nothing, but we had our people and we were working hard. We didn't know it was gonna happen.

ABNER: We were swigging cheap wine.

AMANDA: Yeah. Like literally. How cheap can you buy a bottle of wine for? We'll be taking it.

ABNER: We'll take that one. I will refine my tastes to whatever I can afford.

AMANDA: That's it.

ABNER: Looking back, I can't imagine trusting a person who would tell you to value success over happiness. Like, I can't imagine that's advice anybody would give you. But, essentially, that was what we were hoping for. In a way.

AMANDA: No—we hitched success and happiness together. And they're not. They're not. They're intrinsically not born together. They're not twins at all.

ABNER: Wow. "Success and happiness are not twins."

AMANDA: Yeah, they don't come together.

ABNER: That's so good.

AMANDA: Sometimes they do.

ABNER: You know, when they come together, it's when you have happiness first.

AMANDA: Right. When you have contentment first.

ABNER: You never start with the success and find contentment later. That's rare.

AMANDA: I mean—I don't know. That wasn't our path.

ABNER: That wasn't our path. That's a different book.

AMANDA: That's somebody else's book.

ABNER: "How to Be Successful, Then Find Happiness Later."

AMANDA: Our story was "One Hundred Percent Broke but Happy to Have Our People."

ABNER: When I question God, I remember that in that season, it wasn't that He forced us. He led us right to contentment before He led us to success.

AMANDA: Amen.

ABNER: That refreshes my faith in God.

It's not what I wanted. It's not what we wanted, but it was exactly what we needed.

AMANDA: Right. And if we're ever tempted to doubt His nature by His nos when we've prayed for yeses, it's that season of our life—

ABNER: Wow.

AMANDA: —that says, "Just trust Him."

ABNER: The best answer to prayer I think I've ever had in my life has been no. If we would've gotten all the yeses, who knows what the path would be. But our path has been lined by nos. Honestly, a lot of people say when God closes the door, He opens a window. I don't like that saying. When God closes the door, sometimes, walk away from the damn door.

AMANDA: *[Laughs.]*

ABNER: You're at the wrong door. You're absolutely wasting your time. Right? Move on.

AMANDA: There's actually a garage door open.

ABNER: Or you're at the wrong house. On the wrong block. You know what I mean? Keep walking, keep moving.

AMANDA: I love to think of the nos like bowling bumpers.

ABNER: That's exactly right.

AMANDA: Like, we could have been in the gutter, but the nos just bounced us back and forth until we knocked down some pins. What's crazy about that season is that we had no idea what was coming, how hard the next season would be. We were building this community. It was like we were digging a well, we were digging a foundation for so long. You know, thank God we weren't on the road. We wouldn't have had the community that we have if we'd been gone those couple of years. Instead, we were home and we were broke, and we had nothing else going on. So we had plenty of time to have dinners every Thursday. *We're here. Let's do it.* And that was the net that caught us when we actually went through the hardest season of our life.

ABNER: Right.

AMANDA: That's why community is so important to me. I didn't want us to write separately about the concept of community because I feel like—

ABNER: Community!

AMANDA: Let's have some community in it. I feel like this is how we built JOHN-NYSWIM—not just us as a band, but it's how we built our tour life and it's the reason we're able to bring a sense of home

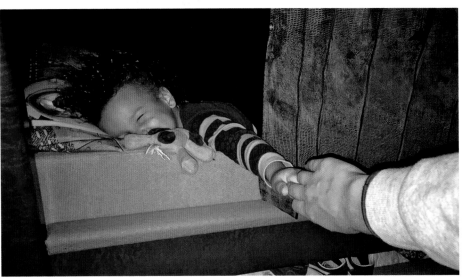

and a sense of unity on tour. We've been on plenty of other tours where there's a bunch of people who all like each other and they hang out and they see each other, but there's not a togetherness. I feel like this community we've built is something we've worked hard to do over the years of touring. And it's something that was birthed out of this season at home where—

ABNER: One hundred percent.

AMANDA: —where that was our focus.

ABNER: Where we learned something we realized we couldn't live without.

AMANDA: Right. In any scenario.

ABNER: Ooh. We had to take home on the road. The road wasn't worth it if home wasn't coming with us.

AMANDA: Exactly.

ABNER: Dang! That's good.

AMANDA: One thing we talked about a lot when we were broke is that money's easy. Plenty of people have money. Money is easy to get. What's harder to get is faith during seasons when you don't have money. What's harder is getting patience.

ABNER: Patience when you're getting a bunch of nos. Like when you're driving in Manhattan, and the lights are timed perfectly so that every light is red. Every light is red as far as you can see. To have faith and to have contentment and true happiness when all you're looking at are red lights? That's hard.

AMANDA: That's valuable.

ABNER: That's valuable. That's worth it.

AMANDA: That's way harder to get than money. That's way harder to get than just success. I feel that community was one of the things that we really dug into and we brought with us on the road. We've had tours where it felt like it wasn't home on the road. It didn't feel like family. It was full of people who were awesome and cool and talented and great. But it was like, *Ah, something's not right.* And we both thought at the end of those tours that maybe we should just stop touring.

ABNER: It's not worth it. But it was the *thing.* The dream was to be on tour all the time. All we wanted to do was that: to be able to play for people. People care about the music we write. To be able to go sing songs to folks, that to me was when I thought we had made it. But, really, we made it when we were broke on a corner in Toluca Lake, L.A., in a little triplex, learning how to build community and learning how to love well and how to build real happiness.

AMANDA: Absolutely. And it's what we do on tours. It's what we do backstage, and it's what we do onstage.

ABNER: Oooh.

AMANDA: It's such an integral part. And one of my favorite things is—

ABNER: Hold on. God was teaching us how to *be* when we were trying to *do*. God forced us into being before he would let us go do the doing.

AMANDA: Yeah.

ABNER: Yeah!

AMANDA: Our community looks like this: Gene making coffee. Berlin teaching Joaquin how to play piano. We were able to invest in community early on in our marriage and early on in JOHNNY-SWIM, and it's something that we've been able to carry with us. It's so integral now when we're at home. Now, when we're on tour, it's something that is across-the-board foundational to who we are as people and who we are as a band. And it's probably my favorite thing about us.

ABNER: Same. We have so many rituals we do on tour now. So many things that are on purpose beyond sound checks, beyond tuning guitars, beyond setup, that are just as important to us as all the things that people see when we're

onstage. Because we realize what we're doing isn't just performing. We're being onstage, and the only way to be our true selves onstage is to be our true selves, period. It's always our goal onstage to build community in that room regardless of your belief system.

AMANDA: Let's commune together.

ABNER: Let's commune together. That's our fight. If we're going to fight for that onstage, we learned, even when we didn't want to, then we have to fight for that offstage, and even on tour, on the tour bus, backstage. We fight for it on days off in hotels. Sometimes we're consciously fighting to commune together.

AMANDA: For sure.

ABNER: We say often that the goal of JOHNNYSWIM is hopefully for people to see us, read this book, and know that it's possible and *worth it* to fight for both your family and your dreams. You fight for your dreams and fight for your family at the same time. You can do both. You can have community and find that as real true success, even when there are other things, like numbers and a career. There are true successes that are even deeper than anything you can hang on a wall, than anything you can show somebody. . . . Hmm. I like this.

[ABNER AND AMANDA HIGH-FIVE.]

I didn't want to do this. I'm glad we did [*laughs*]. Right?

AMANDA: Yeah. I have been excited about having this discussion, 'cause it really is my favorite. I feel like it's been the soil for our marriage. It's been the soil for our work. The soil for our family is communion. Community and communion.

ABNER: Explain that. I like that.

AMANDA: Onstage, our hope is, of course, that we can communicate through a song or an emotion or a feeling or a sense or a thought. That's great. If we can communicate that, that's awesome. And that's one tier. But what we want to do is go beyond that into communion, where we're all partaking of something. Where the moment is bigger than all of us.

ABNER: Ooh. I like that. Hold on. So communicate—good. Community is better.

AMANDA: Right.

ABNER: But the goal is communion.

AMANDA: Where there's something outside of all of us that we all can partake in together, that does something greater in us than it seems like it should do with what's just in our hands.

ABNER: Yeah. It's so good.

AMANDA: It turns into something greater.

ABNER: Come on! It's like yeast, sugar, salt, flour, butter, and water, man. Apart, they're fine. But together, you can make croissants.

AMANDA: [*Laughs.*]

ABNER: And you lose it. You know? At some point when you're eating it, when you have the final product of the croissant, you can't be like, *Oh, here's the yeast, here's the sugar*. It all becomes together a bigger thing.

AMANDA: A bigger thing. And that's what that season was.

ABNER: It was the most dreaded season of my life that I could foretell.

AMANDA: Right.

ABNER: The death of our parents is worse, but you couldn't foretell that. So that season of dread, when we heard from Pastor Dan, who was a prophetic dude. I always kind of trusted his insight into the coming times. He spent a lot of time with us. And he told us this season was coming, a coming season of slowness and contentment. It was the most dreaded thing I'd heard.

AMANDA: It was like a dagger.

ABNER: And I told him, "That's not what I want to hear." As if he's supposed to tell me what I want to hear. And it has been—it has proven itself to be the most valuable season we've ever had. Everything has grown. It's like a vineyard. Remember, we went to Spring Mountain Vineyard, in Napa, with Ron?

AMANDA: Right.

ABNER: I remember Ron was driving us—they had the biggest vineyard in Napa. And Ron said, "Right over there. That's where we grow our premier grapes, our grapes for our most expensive bottle, Elivette. These are our most prestigious vines, right here." And I remember just dumbly saying to him, "Oh, that must be the best soil. That must be the best ground in the whole property." He said, "You know, it's funny. That's the worst ground of the whole property. You see those trees over there? That's the best soil we have. They grow great trees but terrible fruit. Lots of strong branches over there, but nothing you can eat. This soil here, we consciously took away nutrients from it. The soil where our best grapes grow is the soil where the vines had to work the hardest to stay alive." I feel like that season of learning contentment was like the soil in the vineyard—we weren't fighting to stay alive, but we were fight-ing to be happy. We were fighting to find a purpose. We were fighting to find some nutrients. We had to fight for nutrients, because the nutrients—

AMANDA: Didn't just come to us.

ABNER: They didn't just come to us—those things that enriched our lives, even the ones that enriched our bodies. The nutrients were very consciously fought for. We will live forever grateful for that fight for contentment, because it ultimately was a fight for community, a fight for communion. You just can't put a price tag on that. It was the hardest soil to grow in, but it grew in us the most valuable commodity. Our premier grapes, so to speak, our best wine, is our community, and it's something we've learned we can take with us anywhere. Home to go. Home on the road.

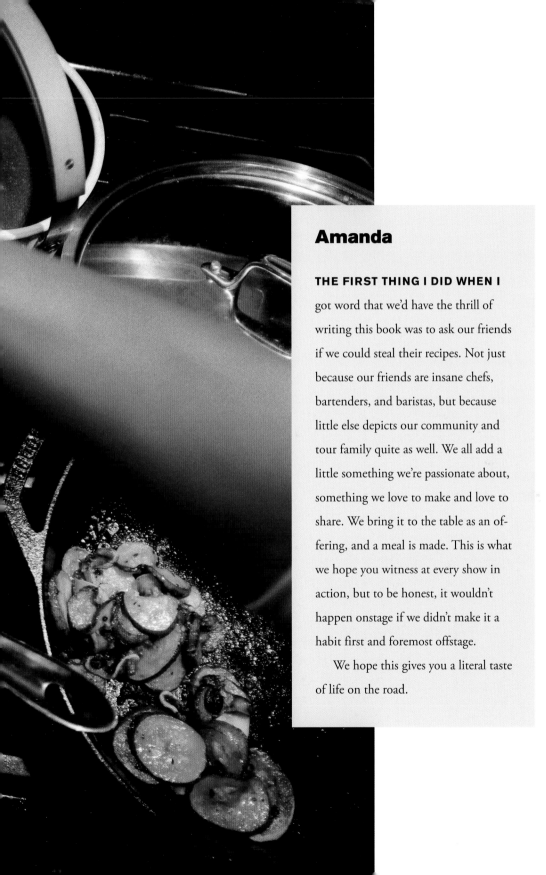

Amanda

THE FIRST THING I DID WHEN I
got word that we'd have the thrill of
writing this book was to ask our friends
if we could steal their recipes. Not just
because our friends are insane chefs,
bartenders, and baristas, but because
little else depicts our community and
tour family quite as well. We all add a
little something we're passionate about,
something we love to make and love to
share. We bring it to the table as an offering, and a meal is made. This is what
we hope you witness at every show in
action, but to be honest, it wouldn't
happen onstage if we didn't make it a
habit first and foremost offstage.

　　We hope this gives you a literal taste
of life on the road.

AMANDA'S HOME FROM TOUR ROAST CHICKEN

It's amazing how well I remember coming home as a kid after being away for a time. More than the weeks of travel, the frequent adventures, and all the beautiful and rare experiences, the thing most etched into my psyche is walking through doors, dropping the bags and itineraries, and welcoming myself back into our haven after feeling tired and hungry and ready for comfort. We were always met with a ready home and fresh sheets. But most important? We were always met with a freshly roasted chicken. As the bird released its aroma while it rested, so did we. Then my family would gather around the table, footsore and hungry, and let her fill us. All of a sudden, once again, we were really home.

To this day, our first home-cooked meal after any tour, long or short, is a simple roasted chicken. Get your meat thermometer and some crunchy bread for dipping ready, folks. You're about to find out what home tastes like.

1 whole chicken
1 onion - peeled; one half sliced
1/2 lemon
olive oil
Salt and pepper

- Preheat oven to 425° and set the chicken on the counter until it gets close to room temperature, around 30-40 min. place in pan.

- Pat the chicky dry and put a small handful of salt in the cavity AKA the "hoo-ha". Put some pepper in there too.

- Stick the half of lemon and half the whole onion in the hoo-ha.

- Sprinkle salt and pepper over the chicken. make sure the breast of the chicken is facing up. Boobies up!

- Drizzle olive oil all over the chicken and rub it around. Then wash your hands because salmonella is gross.

- Place chicken in oven for 20 min, then baste the chicken, put sliced onions around it, and lower temp to 400°.

- Cook for another 30 min then check the temp of the chicken. It should be getting close to 160°. Keep it cooking until it reads between 160-155°.

- Take it out and let it rest for 10-20 min.

- Enjoy your masterpiece.

149

GENE KIM'S COFFEE MOJITO

Gene Kim is our production manager and sound engineer. He's the boss of everything that happens onstage, but on the tour bus he's the boss of keeping everyone caffeinated. At home he has a better espresso setup than the vast majority of American coffee shops, complete with reverse-osmosis water distribution and state-of-the-art Italian machines. He even got our whole tour family into watching barista championships on YouTube after shows, and created what would be his signature drink, sure to win any award. I doubt you've ever had a drink like this in your life. It's part mojito, part iced coffee, and it's amazing. Enjoy your life changing as you sip it.

INGREDIENTS

* Use tall 16 oz cup or Mason Jar
- 7 oz Tonic Water
- 40g or 2oz Single Origin Espresso
- 4-5 mint leaves
- 2 lime wedges
- Ice

INSTRUCTIONS

- Bruise mint & put them at the bottom of your glass.
- Fill cup with ice all the way to the top.
- Squeeze 1 lime wedge over ice.
- Fill glass with tonic H₂O
- Pull Espresso shot & slowly pour over the top.
- Rim glass with lime wedge & garnish.
- Enjoy!

BERLIN'S GRILLED KALE

Jonathan Berlin is a man of an absurd number of talents. It's actually borderline annoying, except he's also so kind and fun that you forget he shouldn't be allowed to be so gifted. He is our musical director, guitar/keyboard/porch-board player, our vinyl-record maker, our songwriting companion, our dear friend. But of his many gifts, the one he is most known for is his grilling expertise, especially in the strangest of circumstances. He's roasted potatoes in a decorative hotel fire pit in Kansas City (unclear are the health implications of this culinary decision, but the potatoes toasted to perfection and tasted delicious), and he has perfected steak and chimichurri cooked on an open flame in many a mall parking lot. The one dish we consistently beg for, regardless of where we are or what else we're cooking, is his grilled kale. I have yet to meet a soul, young or old, who doesn't love it. It's crispy and salty and healthy, and a forever crowd-pleaser.

INGREDIENTS

- CLASSIC CURLY KALE
- FRESH MINCED GARLIC
- COARSE SEA SALT
- THE BEST* RED WINE VINEGAR
- THE BEST* EXTRA VIRGIN OLIVE OIL

SET YOUR GRILL ON HIGH AND WASH YOUR KALE. AFTER THE GRILL IS SCREAMIN' HOT, OPEN THE LID AND LAY OUT THE KALE. QUICKLY DRIZZLE THE OLIVE OIL AND RED WINE VINEGAR OVER THE TOP, BEING MINDFUL OF FIRE FLARE UPS, THEN SEASON BEAUTIFULLY WITH GARLIC AND SALT.

AFTER ABOUT 1 MINUTE, OR AS THE KALE BEGINS TO COLOR AND CHAR, FLIP THE KALE, OIL, VINEGAR, AND SEASON AGAIN. ONCE THE KALE HAS GREAT COLOR AND LOOKS UNDENIABLY DELICIOUS, REMOVE, PLATE, AND EAT IMMEDIATELY. OH, KALE YES...

CHEERS!
BERLIN

* THE BEST IS WHATEVER YOU HAVE IN YOUR KITCHEN!

151

DARREN LAU'S
LAVENDER WHISKEY SOUR

Darren Lau is our resident bartender (and therapist and chef and spiritual guru and photographer and onetime electric bill payer and he designed this page). This is one of his signature drinks. The lavender will calm all your worries right alongside the whiskey. It's a killer combo. Literally everyone likes this drink, which is both awesome and dangerous.

MAKES TWO DRINKS
4.5 oz RYE WHISKEY
1 LEMON
0.75 oz HONEY
1 EGG WHITE
LAVENDER BITTERS

INSTRUCTIONS

1 THROW WHISKEY, LEMON JUICE, & HONEY TO SHAKER

2 ADD IN EGG WHITE AND SHAKE FOR 15-30 SECONDS

3 ADD ICE AND SHAKE AGAIN FOR 30 SECONDS

4 POUR INTO TWO CUPS

5 ADD 3 DASHES OF BITTERS

AMY WATERS'S APPLE PIE

Amy Waters is an actual angel sent from above. In the summer of 2017, right before I got pregnant with Luna, she started traveling with us and watching Joaquin. Life had begun to change so much, so quickly, and wasn't slowing down. We had prayed for someone to help us through transitions and make home on the road special and awesome for Joaquin while we're busy working. Prayers answered. Not only does she make it fun on the road, but she is also a pro at making home feel just as fun and safe when we're traveling as when he's at home in California. Which brings me to, drumroll please: Amy's Apple Pie. This is her family's recipe that she is so kindly sharing with us here. It's delicious and warming, the perfect comfort food for when life is exactly as it should be but especially for when life is a little uncomfortable and abnormal. Amy and Joaquin often make it while we're gone, but they're kind enough to save us a slice or two to welcome us home, which is good because this pie never lasts long.

The Crust
1 1/2 cups flour
1 tsp salt
1/2 cup corn oil
1 1/2 tsp sugar
2 tbsp cold milk
Mix together and flatten in pie pan

The Filling
3/4 cup sugar
1/4 cup all-purpose flour
1/2 tsp nutmeg
1/2 tsp cinnamon
Dash of salt
6 cups thinly sliced apples
   (about 6 medium)

The Topping
1 cup all purpose flour
1/2 cup cold butter
1/2 cup brown sugar

1. Heat oven to 425°
2. Mix sugar, flour, nutmeg, cinnamon, and salt
3. Mix in apples
4. Put apple mix in prepared crust
5. Sprinkle the topping to cover apples
6. Bake 35-40 minutes
7. Cover pie with foil and bake another 10 minutes
8. You did it!
   Now go eat it while it's warm
   ♡ Amy

Abner

"Do you know a cure for me?"
"Why, yes," he said. "I know of a cure for everything. Salt water."
"Salt water?" I asked him.
"Yes," he said, "in one way or the other. Sweat, or tears, or the salt sea."
—Karen Blixen, Seven Gothic Tales

WHEN I THINK OF MY FATHER, I see the sea.

Expansive but not without limits. A tapestry woven in contradictions: fear and peace, life and death. The same sea's waves crash against cliffs and gently lap the shore. That was my father.

When I speak to my father in dreams, it's always a bit odd because usually he's a cardboard cutout or sick or just about to leave—enough to offer a clue of his absence in waking life. But as I awake, I am reminded that even his absence is now as much a part of his legacy and influence on me as his presence was.

He is legend.

My father lived with a wild and bold heart, held out in front of him everywhere he went, welcoming scars ruthlessly while engulfing every surrounding with passion. He was fearless. He was true. Always knowing his true north, he saw things clearly, steady like the horizon. There was right and there was wrong, and never the twain shall meet.

When I think of my father, I see the

LET IT MATTER

horizon and see the line that is always true regardless of the battles faced within the waters. As a pastor, as a poet, as a father, husband, and friend, the line was always clear with my dad. No matter the battles that raged within and around him, he was always true. Always steady. He is legend.

I envision how he must have seen the Caribbean as he was about to take his entire family on a dangerous ninety-mile sprint that would either end their lives or change them forever: *bold*. My father prayed before that boat launched, and all the prisoners and folks from the insane asylum who were smuggled on by the Cuban government mocked him as he did. But he arrived at "Amen" no more quickly. Then, a few days into what should have taken merely hours, as the storm shook the little vessel with no land in sight, all those same hardened and grisly men cried out: *"Priest, pray for us! Priest, pray for us!"* My father's reply was simply, "No," then, "I already prayed we'd arrive safely. Now I have faith that prayer will be answered."

When I think of my father, I see the sea.

When I think of my father, I see his sweat.

The trophy of a hard day's work. There was joy in his sweat, a knowing that he set out to do a thing. And whether it was accomplished or not, he set himself

to it in full. I can't remember ever seeing my dad sweaty and sad. With him, there was always joy attached to hard work. His biceps weren't huge or anything, but those freckled dark arms always seemed to be stronger than they should have been and slick from exertion. I remember how much harder he could work than I could. The man got fat and got old, and still he could somehow load a truck, rebuild the roof of an old church, fix the engine, work the lawn, help someone move, with more will (and, frankly, more joy) than I was ever able to build up.

Dad was determined in everything he did. Even if his objective was to wait, he would set to it with fierceness. I'll leave that for another book, but Dad had to wait a lot. To get out of Cuba, they waited on the shore for days, then on the dock for days, then on the boat for days. That was all after years of waiting for the opportunity to get out in the first place. He waited to find work, but when he got it, he set his whole self to it. When he was taken from us for those twelve years (another book *entirely*), he waited, never taking the easy way out. Always with dogged determination, he'd wait.

I see him praying for me from that prison cell when I was six years old, and hear him shout, *"Lord! My son! My son!"* Sweat and tears mingled on his beautiful face. His only son, being raised miles

away by four women, while they all had no choice but to wait. From where he sat, distance wasn't counted in miles but in years. Sweat on his brow. Determined.

He prayed faithfully for me every day. He'd call us every day at 5:00 P.M., and we'd split the time in that collect call between us: fifteen minutes to Mom and fifteen minutes between my sisters and me. Every day. For twelve years. The truest man I have ever known. The hardest-working, most ferocious person I've ever met. Even in his passing, I see him on that hospital bed intubated, with small chance at recovery, shaking loose his right leg from the sheets, shaking it next to his bed, trying to get up and take himself to the bathroom.

When I think of my father, I see his sweat.

• • •

When I think of my father, I see his tears.

I remember that last morning, joining him at 9:00 A.M. on the living room floor, where he often slept because of his back pain. Dad rarely slept past 5:00 A.M. I heard Mom talking to him, and I heard him struggling to speak. I remember the fear. I remember kneeling at his side and holding his face between my hands, shouting at him, *"Papi, Papi, quien soy yo!?"* "Daddy, Daddy, who am I?" I remember his broken English and the tears as he said, "You are my son, Abner Pedro."

Dad was the greatest storyteller. If I have become a professional musician partly because of my use of words, it's only because I got to listen to him tell stories. Sure, he'd tell the same stories over and over and over and over. But when I tell you that he would cry at precisely the same moment in each story every time and that absolutely none of it was false, I mean it. He meant it. Every time.

I remember when he once again told Amanda a story he had told her at least a bajillion times before. All my nieces and nephews were in the room while Dad was telling the emotional story. I've got seven beautiful nieces and nephews in Jacksonville, Florida, who all love their "Titi Panda" very much and are loved deeply in return. They were *all* vying for her attention as Dad dove into his story. I might as well have gotten out the pop-

corn, because one thing about Dad's storytelling is that he had no time for people who didn't give him 100 percent of their attention. So I watched, hella amused, as Amanda tried not to break eye contact with Dad while seven wild ones tried to get her to respond to them. *Here it comes, the part where he breaks.* He always cried at this point . . . almost . . . almost . . . *"Titi Panda! Titi Panda! Titi Panda! Titi Panda! Titi Panda!!!!!"* She turned for half a second to quiet the little ones. That half a second was too long. Dad turned to me with that unreleased tear still in his eye and said in Spanish, "Why do I even try to tell her this story if she's not going to pay attention?!" He got up and went into the kitchen to make coffee.

Ha! She, of course, knew the rest of the story because she'd heard it so often. But Dad still always cried at that point.

He always cried at the parts where he'd talk about his daddy.

He was strong but wasn't ashamed to cry. If it mattered, *it mattered.* He was the picture of perseverance, showing me by example that often the best way over is through.

When I think of my father, I see his tears.

Too few words that took too long to write. Damn I miss him.

Amanda

GRIEF IS A WEIGHTED WING. RE- gardless of whether you find yourself soaring over trees or stumbling on a sidewalk, life always feels heavier once you've carried loss. You can still fly, and it often makes you stronger, but the ease is gone. There is no youthful ignorance or denial of mortality when someone so close to you dies in their prime, full of life, hope, dreams, beauty, and jokes. (Cue "Do You Realize" by The Flaming Lips.)

Losing my mother was a tornado we didn't see coming. One moment, we were watching a gorgeous sunset, the next moment the neighborhood flagpole was in our living room and our roof was on the neighbor's lawn. No matter how familiar we might be with death on this earth, it still feels like a distant stranger. For something so natural, nothing feels less.

It's not lost on me that I found out my mother was sick on April 1, the date people play horrible pranks on one another. The day felt like a cruel joke. It still does. As we finished writing the song "Annie" in a little writers' room in Nashville, my phone rang. It was my sister, Brooklyn. With a steadied voice, she told me the news. The results of my mother's tests had come back, the ones we had disregarded as being precautionary. Turns

out she was right to get tested. She had stage-four cancer.

All it took was one sentence for my faith to collapse and, apparently, my lungs with it. I wept so hard, I couldn't breathe, let alone speak. I had never gotten a call like this, but I'll be honest: I thought I would do better. I thought I would be stronger and braver, but I was a shell of my best self. I was primal in my devastation. I flew directly home the next morning. It was the second-worst flight of my life.

We did all the things you do when you get this sort of news. We prayed and cried and laughed through aching chests. We researched and googled and gained hope and lost hope and gained it again. We went through all the stages of grief multiple times a day. All day. Every day. Until the day we lost her. And now, eight years later, we still roll through them . . . denial then anger then bargaining then depression then acceptance, just more loosely, more slowly, and with more recognition.

A little over a year after the phone call that changed my life, on Mother's Day 2012, I flew to Florida to see her. A short ten months earlier, we had lost Omar, and three weeks earlier, my grandmother.

The tornadoes kept coming. I bought the flight when we still had hope, when I thought seeing my mom would bring me more joy than sorrow, and long before we knew it would be the end. She had been doing well for a while. But cancer is a demon with lots of sneaky tricks. The doctors said she had only days left.

I spent most of the five hours on the plane writing her Mother's Day card. She absolutely loved cards. She could spend four hours, easily, at a Hallmark store (do they even exist anymore?), but only for the funny ones. She couldn't handle sappy sentiments. So I wrote her the sappiest few paragraphs I've ever written on the funniest card I could find. It seemed like a good compromise. I quietly wept, not wanting the random folks in my row to notice. I used every bit of space on that dumb stock paper trying to adequately thank her, love her, honor her. It could never be enough, but it was all I knew to do. It was the worst flight of my life.

She left us on a stormy night while I slept a few doors down, and then the whirlwind started. Planning a funeral is just like planning a wedding, only while emotionally traumatized and with only three days to do it all. Who knew? The hardest part is knowing what to say and how to respond to all the love and sorrow aimed in your direction. You're already

underwater. You can look up and see the trees and the sky, and you know there is a world out there, but you can't hear much, and everything is blurry. You wobble back and forth between panic and a lifeless float, all the while trying to manage the kindness of others, which can easily turn into a burden if left unsupervised.

Condolences come with a side of beige casserole. Comfort food speaks louder than words in these times, and, believe it or not, it's easier to digest than the "She's in a better place" comments. The truth of statements like these is one thing, but processing it can be difficult. I juggled emotions, hoping to find a rhythm between extreme gratitude, aching disappointment, and the sharp sting of loss, but no one really teaches you how to do this. Growing up in a faith-filled home taught me a lot of amazing things and built in me some of my most treasured attributes, but no one taught me how to grieve. Maybe it felt too close to disbelief or a lack of faith. I don't know. Maybe we communally thought that if we just ignored it, we would never have to face it.

One morning my phone buzzed with a text alert. It was from a dear friend, Rachel Jonas. She had lost her father the year before and was fresh in the earth of grief herself. The text was only two sentences long: *Suffer. She was worth it.*

Suddenly there was space for my grief. It was the permission I needed to not rush to try to superglue my broken heart. It would take time and honesty, and that was not only okay, it was necessary. It wasn't a lack of faith or a denial of joy. My suffering was proof of both. It was proof of the gift I'd received in such a wonderful mother and of the immense joy and abundance her life had brought us.

I don't know who said the following, but I learned this to be true: You cannot deaden the pain and still discover joy. You cannot numb your heart and still know how to hurt and heal. If you can hold the sorrow and the joy together, over time the sorrow can become fertilizer for the joy to grow. It still stinks, but the fruit and the flowers are worth it.

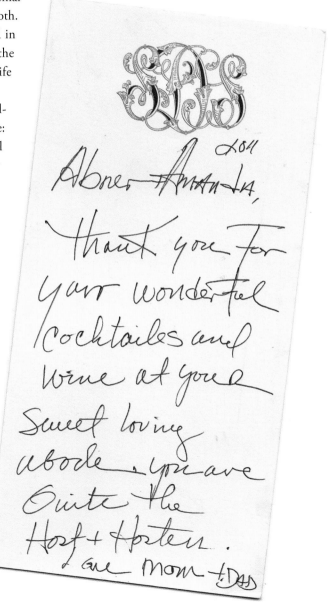

Amanda

AS LONG AS I CAN REMEMBER, two words have haunted me. Even as a child, ignorant of the full extent of their meaning, the shameful feeling these words left in my gut was visceral and deep. I couldn't fully define them, but I could fully feel them. Like bullies, these words reminded me, within a whisper of hearing them, that I was always on the precipice of being unlovable and, ultimately, worthless. And, like skeletons, they left me scared and panicked, even though they had no real meat on them. Maybe you have felt them stalking as well. Prepare yourself. I'm about to say them. Don't let them trigger you. The words . . . here they come. . . .

Mediocre and *lazy.*

Oof. They sound gross, don't they? I'm shocked *mediocre* doesn't count as onomatopoeia. The word drips with the disdain it creates. *Lazy* does, too, actually. Guess what? I've been avoiding writing this section for days, which is perfect because now we can let this be a case study in real time as you read of the exhausting loop I get caught in.

Here we go. An hour ago, the kids went down for a nap. The house was quiet. The time was finally right. I decided I was going to start writing, but instead I cleaned the bathroom. For some reason

it needed to be disinfected immediately. Afterward, I got out my computer and opened this page. It was blank and limitless. Terrifying. Good thing right then I received an "important" text, so I responded. Somehow, one thing led to another, and I wound up on Instagram. A tale as old as time. It's all the Internet's fault.

This is when the internal dialogue revs up.

I'm not a writer, and I'm a horrible storyteller. People are going to be bored.

The downward spiral begins.

I don't even know what I want to say yet, so maybe I should just sit and think about it for a while.

The vortex strengthens.

Also, it's probably not that great an idea, and if it was, I probably wouldn't do it justice, and I think I need coffee and I think I'm dehydrated and I don't even know what I want to say, plus dinner needs to get going, so I probably won't get anything done anyway.

See? This inner voice feels like an annoying big sister who uses a lot of run-on sentences. She has a point sometimes (dinner probably should get in the oven, and I do need coffee), but she blinds me to the ultimate truth of life, which is you have to be mediocre for a while before you can be great.

This dizzying and unfortunate habit might seem like nothing more than procrastination. I used to think that's all it was, but it's weightier than that. The root of this creative hostage situation is fear. Not a fear of failure but a fear of being average, a fear of that disgusting thing known as mediocrity. *That* is the thing that will paralyze you. Give me fear of failure any day. I know how to fix that. You just run to the edge of the cliff and jump off. But the fear of being good when great is looming, when excellence is what you really want? That is murky water. It's the Everglades. It's got monsters and dead bodies floating around.

The problem is that if there is a gene for laziness, I for sure have it. Doing nothing feels very natural to me. I'm not a perfectionist, and while I do have a competitive bone or two, achieving more than necessary is not really my thing. I used to post scriptural warnings against laziness around my bedroom and on my mirrors with a dry-erase marker. It was my form of self-flagellation. But like most of our bad habits, laziness was something I couldn't guilt my way out of. So there I was. Stuck between a rock and a very comfortable soft place I wanted to nap in.

The thing is: I am greedy. I don't want to be pretty good. I want to wow myself, I want to wow others with my talent and expertise at the things I love. Not for the applause, but for the passion. I want to battle against *good* in the quest for *great*. I want to prove to life that I'm worth it. But that greed suffocates me. It undermines and distracts me from what matters. It rots the roots. When I don't feel like I'm achieving what I think I should, all progress ceases. Fear of mediocrity and laziness play catch with me. They toss me back and forth. No one wins.

So, for those of you readers who find yourself in these words, I'm with you. I have no panacea. We will be bad at things for a little while, and then we will be good, just plain good, for a very long while, until finally, maybe, we get a little great. It doesn't seem like a fantastic deal, but greatness isn't a cheap date. And we shouldn't want it to be. It's worth fighting for, patiently and consistently. It's worth wooing with your time and attention.

My mom used to say that often in life we feel like we're going in circles, seeing the same things over and over, but it's not just a circle. It's a spiral. We go round and round, but we're moving up, our perspective growing with each turn.

So let's do this. Let's be okay with being okay. We got this. Keep moving forward. I'll meet you at the top.

Amanda

JOHNNYSWIM NEVER SKYROCK-eted. What's the opposite of an overnight success? We were more like that. There were a lot of side jobs (I can both make you a latte and deal you blackjack) and a few late bills (we still owe Darren Lau two hundred dollars for that electric bill we couldn't pay in 2012), but after years of going it more or less alone, we finally had a small team of champions surrounding and guiding us: our manager, Jay King, and our first booking agent, Bobby Cudd.* They believed in us, took a chance, and were willing to passionately work on our behalf when others just sort of juggled and fumbled us.

Jay offered himself as our manager for free for a whole year before ever taking a paycheck. Bobby used whatever professional capital he had in his decades-long career to get us slots at festivals or into little venues in towns where no one had ever heard of us. Rolling out his big map and sharpening his pencil, Bobby routed us around the country, introducing us to all his promoter friends and colleagues.

Meanwhile, Jay painstakingly scoured each of those cities for hidden opportunities, like radio stations or marketing offices or anywhere else where we could try to woo people in person. We were a ragtag group of dreamers.

To say Jay and Bobby honored us with their guidance, creativity, expertise, and love is an understatement. In an unstable industry that often quakes, crumbles, or waits for someone else to make the first move down a well-beaten path, these two helped pave a bespoke way for us. The chains on the bike locked into gear; finally the wheels weren't just spinning anymore. It was slow and steady, but we were going somewhere for once.

We drove ourselves to shows in vans, but now, with Bobby booking the gigs, people were actually going to show up. People we didn't know! We were playing for real-life strangers just like we'd always hoped! It was a miracle! We plodded along show by show, city by city. Then back again, show by show, city by city.

* There's no real good place to put this, but we would be remiss not to include this story to help you understand the brilliance of Bobby Cudd. We were at Bonnaroo in 2013. We were playing four or five sets in a row on different small stages at the festival one day. We were starving and were what seemed like miles away from any of the food stalls. In precisely the deepest moment of starvation, a miracle happened. Bobby Cudd, who'd been traveling stage to stage with us for at least five hours, noticed our sour demeanor and pulled two hot dogs out of his pocket. *Out of his pocket!* They had the works on them, too. How long had those been in there? No one asked. Our hunger ended. Never doubt Bobby Cudd to get the job done.

THANK YOU
THE TONIGHT SHOW WITH JAY LENO

Then back again. Then back again. We took our time, and before long, strangers were even bringing their stranger friends. We stayed on the road three hundred days a year, falling in love with cities and restaurants and people, becoming somewhat addicted to the pace of it all. It wasn't easy, but we made it fun. We counted the pains as a fair price for getting to build our dang dream with our own dang dream team.

After a few tours, we were able to hire a band to take with us. These guys believed in us as well, enough to take pay cuts and leave home and help lay bricks with us on this thing we were building. It was an honor to have them, and it was so much freakin' fun. We became family, glorified roommates, comfortable complaining about who left the toilet seat up and whose suitcase exploded over every hotel room. We all knew who snored, [*coughs*] Berlin [*coughs*], who was a safe driver, and who only drove when at least two others were awake and watching the road, who told the best jokes (if you're looking for "that's what she said" jokes, I'm for sure your girl there), who sang the best karaoke song, and whose mom sent us away from hometown visits with the best snacks. The type of community we lovingly built at home formed on the road. Despite the sacrifices, we shared a deep knowing we got to spend our days doing what we loved with whom we loved, and that's about as good as it gets. We knew we were lucky. Tired, but lucky.

As the momentum built, so did my age. Yikes. No girl wants to think about her eggs slowly shriveling up like little microscopic dust bunnies, but there I was, noticing the gentle tick-tock of my biological clock getting louder. We knew we wanted kids; we wanted a bunch. But no time ever seemed right. In my perfect imaginary world, kids made sense later, when we could afford private jets and multiple nannies, obviously. Some dear friends who traveled with their baby told us that babies are portable, but I was suspicious. These friends didn't work in clubs for a living and, unfortunately, there is no chapter for touring parents in *Babywise,* so I was still very unsure of how it would work logistically.

Rowdy late nights in overpacked rooms soaked with years of beer, smoke, and questionable body fluids followed by sluggish early mornings of travel after a few hours of sleep on a crunchy hotel bed while a bandmate snored in the other bed. Another early morning, another free hotel breakfast, another dirty backstage, another late show, another cheap chain hotel. The food was often fast, the drives often slow, and the car always packed. So packed, in

fact, that Abner and I dedicated ourselves to traveling as long as possible with the smallest suitcase possible. We were going weeks with one small carry-on.

Traveling with a baby and all its stuff in tow seemed downright impossible.

Every night post-show was a sweaty, hours-long game of Tetris. All the guys stood staring into an empty trunk, tailgate open, gear and suitcases piled around them. I sat on the curb counting merch and making sure we hadn't gotten robbed (or, more likely, that Abner didn't give away too much). Then we'd shove the boxes of counted merch here, push guitars along the edge there, stack drums just so here and there, hide suitcases under this seat or that cymbal case. The guys would get it down to a science just in time for the leg of that tour to be over and a new one to begin in a different city and in a different rental car. The thought of adding in even one more variable like, say, a car seat, sounded overwhelming at best. In fact, when people would ask when we were going to start a family, I'd say, "When babies can safely be placed in the overhead bin." I was clearly not ready for motherhood.

But then, without much warning, it happened. I got knocked up. Does anyone ever find out they're pregnant and not feel shocked? Even if you're trying for a baby, new life always feels like a stunning new miracle. Probably because it is. I'd be lying if I said there wasn't a solid level of panic on the surface, but underneath I was thrilled. Yes, there were a million unknowns. Where would the baby sleep on tour, who would watch it while I was on stage, how much coffee is too much for breast milk? Luckily, humans take a long freaking while to make, and by the time our magnificent Joaquin came along, most of those crooked edges straightened right out.

I couldn't imagine life on the road with a baby the way we had been traveling, but turns out I didn't need to. Just in the nick of time, suddenly, we could afford a tour bus for tours. We no longer needed to drive hours on end between shows. Now we could cuddle up after a show and our nightly game of gear Tetris, have a drink, go to sleep, and wake up rested where we needed to be. It was a wild upgrade. And just in time.

Our first bus showed up at the very first Christmas show we played in Nashville, in 2014. I was eight months pregnant. I waddled myself and my belly, in the cold, to the front of the bus, pulling the weighty door open. Immediately, the scent of the front lounge rushed at me. All bus companies must use the same cleaning stuff, because all at once I was a kid, climbing up the steps into one of my mom's buses. But this time, it was for my own shows

and my own tour. How was that even real? I toured our little temporary home with tears cresting, because nostalgia and hormones are a helluva mix. It was cozy and clean. And sure enough, in the way back of the bus, there was a bed big enough for Abner and me (and my belly, which needed its own two pillows and three feet of space). Right next to the bed was an area the perfect size for a crib.

Joaquin was born a couple of months later, and joined us on his first tour when he was around five weeks old. His crib fit perfectly in the back, and he slept there until he was big enough for his own bunk with the big guys. He learned to crawl on a towel-covered, stained-green floor in Charlotte, and to walk in the bus's front lounge in Madison, Wisconsin. I wouldn't have been able to imagine this life. But it works, and it is wonderful.

This sort of thing has happened time and again in our life and career. We leap off the cliff and a step magically appears, just like in *Indiana Jones*. We don't think we're quite ready, but we take a step anyway: Our team emerges out of thin air after we spend years waiting, the tour bus shows up at the same time as the babies, and the babies end up being portable after all. Miraculously, the ground is always beneath us. We just have to keep taking those wonderfully scary steps.

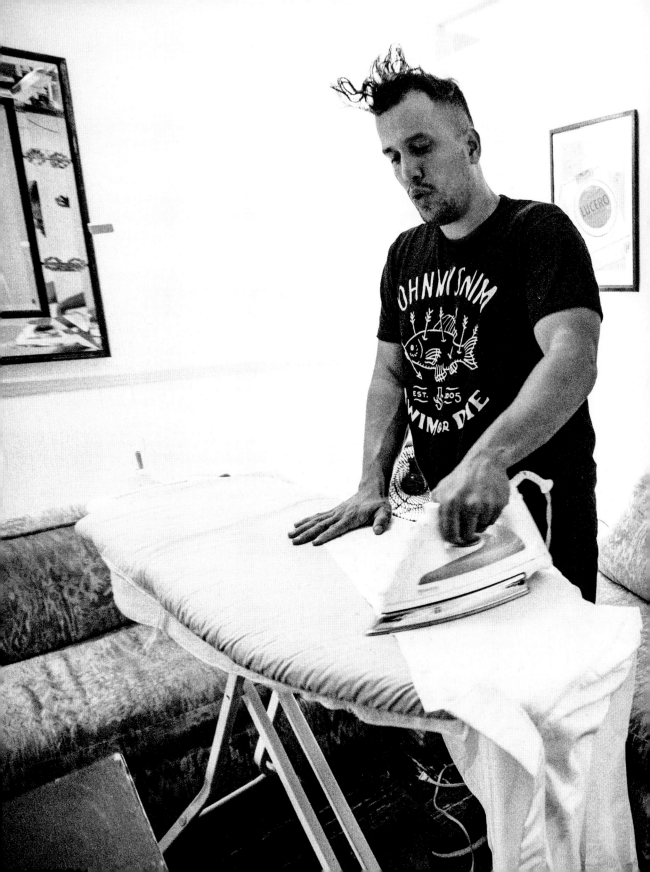

AMANDA: I think from the beginning we wanted a team. As nice as it sounded to be under some bigwig manager, somebody who would be our champion and somebody who could do all-powerful things, I think what we really wanted was a team, so that we could form something ourselves. We wanted to have our hands in the clay of this thing we were building, to get our hands dirty and messy, and be proud of what we came up with. We didn't want to just be like, *Here, I'm a lump of clay—*

ABNER: Make me famous!

AMANDA: Yeah.

JAY: And that was my attraction to you. You could tell that you knew who you were. You had been through it. You had shed that skin. You had this . . . It wasn't cockiness. It was the confidence that said none of that actually mattered. What mattered was the *intention* behind what you did. In my line of work, that was rare.

ABNER: We'd had all the meetings and all the meals. The readers have heard me say this a couple of times. The old mentality a lot of artists had was that they were looking to be rescued: *Give me the person, the connections, to rescue me and take me to the mountaintop.* And I love

what you're saying, Jay. You're saying it's shedding that skin. That was the skin we shed. That ideal [of being rescued]—it really was an ideal, and a goal—that said, *You'll meet that one person. Maybe it will be the guy who broke so-and-so. Maybe it will be this person, maybe it will be this mega-manager.* And for me, it was shed in a rough way through my first contract, which I won't dwell on here. I was able to learn a lot of that through Amanda's parents. That's really, I think, the greatest asset Amanda gained from her parents. It wasn't about their connections. It was the intimate knowledge and wisdom she got to gain without having to live through the bad experiences I had.

AMANDA: Right.

ABNER: So, when Amanda and I met you, Jay, we'd known you a little bit. We'd connected. But in that moment, we were putting the pieces together that we should work together. We met in a moment where we realized we didn't want somebody who could pick us up and take us to the mountaintop. We wanted somebody who could look up at the mountain, strap a backpack on, put their head to the wind, and say, "All right, let's go." We were trying to add somebody to us. And I really think that's what we found in you. We realized that what we really

needed was a partner for the ride—not somebody who was going to rescue us.

JAY: The first thing I remember is that photo shoot you guys did in the kitchen, before we ever met. It's a moment that has never left me. Mike McGlaflin [Amanda's brother-in-law and all around JOHNNYSWIM creative and career aide] came into my office and was like, "Yo, I'm gonna play you these songs. And check this photo shoot out."

ABNER: I think that might have been the second photo shoot we ever did.

AMANDA: It was probably in 2007.

JAY: I was working as an A&R [artists and repertoire] guy in Christian music. No offense to the industry, but it wasn't something I wanted to do. It was just kind of where my path had landed. I remember after hearing those songs and seeing the photo shoot, I thought, *Why can't I be involved in that? Why can't I sign somebody like that?* It had nothing to do with a hit song or the top of the charts. It was something that felt genuine. It was authentic. It was real. When I would hear

179

your music and see who you were and what you did, it all kind of made sense to me. And it always stayed there. You may not realize that this was something I'd been dreaming about. I was in a job, providing for my family, but my heart, my soul, everything I wanted from my childhood in music wasn't there for me. Mike would encourage me as a friend—he's been a big brother to me since I met him over twenty years ago. So he was always like, "Dude, if you want to do this, I'll make the hookup."

AMANDA: We'd already had some memorable "hookups."

ABNER: Remember, we met with this big, big mega-manager? I don't even want to remember his name [name intentionally omitted]. You know, he's not the biggest in the business now, but he was then.

JAY: He's still a big name.

ABNER: He had this huge brownstone on Central Park West. I remember, we sat down and it was like he was putting on this show. He was on a phone call and made us wait awhile. Then finally we sat down and he was in a rush. "Play me something, play me some music." We played him a song. "Okay, that's fine. You got more?" "No, that's all we really got right now." Then he looked at Amanda and said, "Your name is Sudano? Huh. Amanda Sudano. You're gonna have to change that. That's not a good name. That's not gonna work." Amanda looked at him and said, "Excuse me, what's your name?"

AMANDA: I honestly didn't really know his name.

ABNER: A super famous manager at the time. A *huge* name, and she's all, *What's your name?* He says his name. She goes, "Sounds like trash to me. You better change that name. *[Laughter.]* I'm ready to go. Abner, how about you?"

AMANDA: That situation clearly didn't work out. *[Laughter.]*

ABNER: She literally got up and walked out. And I'm the super-young, very-impressed-at-all-this artist. I'm like, "Okay, sir, I guess we're leaving."

AMANDA: I'm like, "We're out." But that's the thing, growing up I had all these people, all these bigwigs, with all the ego and all the attitude. And I was like, "I'm good. I'm happy to work at Starbucks and get to do what I love with people I love versus doing whatever you say and not being able to have any say over my life."

ABNER: Right. And I think—Amanda, correct me if I'm wrong—from your perspective, because of all these people you had access to, you got to see managers and label guys who were these super famous, wealthy folks, and they just kept having this cycle of artists they were working through. Like the manager who'd been famous forever but had thirty artists you'd never heard of and was clinging to that one hit song. I feel like, knowing you now, that's so unattractive. I don't want the famous man with one hundred unknown artists and the one famous song or whatever. Like, "It ain't about you, sir. I'm good now."

JAY: I remember, we met, then Abner and I kept in touch. That photo of you guys in the kitchen and the song I heard never left my mind. I kept thinking to myself, *Why can't we do something like that?* We kept having little meetings, until that one time at Jonathan's restaurant in Franklin, Tennessee, when we finally sat down—

ABNER: It was just you and me, and I remember you said, "Listen, obviously what you guys do doesn't fit with where I am with my situation at my job right now. You guys aren't a Christian band. But I would love to work with you. And I'd be willing to work for you guys for free for a year. . . . I don't know if you want everybody to know this, because maybe young artists—

JAY: No, it's fine. I was moonlighting, bro. Actually, it's one of the things that got me fired, to be honest with you. I think the head of the label got a little jealous because we started to get some steam, and then everybody on the staff was talking. But I was like, *I'm kind of miserable. I know I need to make a change.* We met in Nashville, and I wasn't even living in Nashville. I was trying to get back and figure out how to do it. I remember thinking, *All right, I've spent ten years plus in one industry. If I do this, I'm going to be taking a step back. I'm going to be resetting the entire thing.* I knew it was going to be another ten-year journey. I didn't sign up thinking this [JOHNNYSWIM] was a one-hit wonder. I didn't sign up thinking this was going to be a fast rocket ship. I signed up with the thought of literally ten years in my mind. I was like, *I wanna see this all the way through.*

AMANDA: Well, here we are! Eight years running, at least.

JAY: People ask, "How did you do this? What happened? What is this?" I tell this to people all the time. I say there are two central keys. I just told this to an artist yesterday—I said, I think it was a combination of two things. One is that you had

a group of people in Abner, Amanda, and Jay that had been there, seen it, whether it was a record deal, whether it was people taking meetings, etcetera. I mean, we'd done all that stuff. You know, we'd done the fancy offices. We'd done the fancy meals. I had worked for all these different things. You guys had done all this stuff. And we eventually realized none of that equaled anything at the end of the day. There was a lot of time and a lot of energy spent. It was fun to get a free meal, especially when you're broke. You're like, *Yo, we're definitely running up the tab tonight.*

ABNER: It's like the meals were the one thing that kept me from being super hungry: *I might get a contract and we're gonna get dessert? Okay by me.*

JAY: Yeah. You're like, all right, let's keep going. Let's have another drink. So I think we had shed that skin in our lives. That was one key. And then the second key was the trust factor that we have had. We look at each other in an equal way on this journey. I trust you guys and your instinct. You trust me and my instinct. When you have that, it feels unstoppable. It's not like, "I am the manager and you are my artist." And you guys aren't like, "That's the manager who's gonna get me everything, and I'm the artist." I think that's probably the biggest problem with

artists and a big problem with managers. What did we always say? We would say this on our jogs together. We'd agree, "We need to be setting the pace." Right? So we made a decision that we were going to set the pace. Now that might not be popular. It might not be something that everybody wants to do or think, or it's not easy. Sometimes you've got to say no. A lot of times artists think that they're gonna sign a booking deal, a manager, etcetera. And the pace that manager sets is gonna be what they run. And if it doesn't work, then they blame the manager, and vice versa. The manager, a lot of times, says, "Well, you're the artist, write a hit song, set the pace for me so I can be successful." We didn't have that. But I think it's because of the first point: We had shed so much of our skin. It's almost like we were young, but still had grown up at that point where we were colliding with our mature selves and could say, "Okay, we trust our instincts. We're also teachable. Flexible. We're adjustable."

ABNER: Yeah, man. One hundred percent.

JAY: Here's something I never forget: Somebody told me a long time ago that the key to success a lot of the time is *adjustment*. You either are going to adjust or you're going to be adjusted. One way or another, life's going to do that to you. I remember when I met you guys, I needed an adjustment moment. I was providing for my family. I was the head of A&R, but I wasn't happy. The job wasn't fulfilling. My soul wasn't fulfilled. I thought, *This isn't where I want my legacy to go.* So I thought, *All right, I'm either going to be adjusted out of this situation or I'm going to make the adjustment.* When we met

at Jonathan's, I was like, "I'm in." But I didn't know what the hell I was talking about.

ABNER: We didn't have a booking deal. We didn't have a record deal.

AMANDA: So you're sitting there at Jonathan's, and we're like, "Yes, high-five, we're going to do this together!" Like you said, it's not like management is over here and the artist is over there. We're all together, like one big, happy family. I think Abner talks to you some days more than he talks to me. And that might be a real statistic.

ABNER: Yeah, for sure.

JAY: My wife feels the same.

ABNER: I remember—when I was attending Trevecca Nazarene University for that one year, before I got kicked out—I took a music business course with a legend named Jim Foglesong. He's since passed away, but he was a legend in the business. He had the biggest class on campus. It was in a small theater, a couple hundred kids per class. I don't remember anything except for one thing from Jim Foglesong's class. There was so much practical stuff he taught that literally from that moment in 2001 to now in 2020 should be put in a history class, not in a music business class, because the industry doesn't work that way anymore. One thing he said always stuck with me. He said, "The second-closest relationship you'll have as an artist in your entire life will be your manager. The first will be your wife, your husband, or your significant other. Then it'll be your manager, then it'll be your mom, and move on from there." And I remember that got a laugh. I was an eighteen-year-old freshman in college. Everybody kind of chuckled, like he was joking. And if that hasn't proven itself to be written in stone for us. For me, it's Amanda. It's Jason Scott King. It's Marisol Ramirez. And then we can move on from there.

AMANDA: That's how it works. But I'm wondering. For me, it felt like we were trudging along. Trucking? Trudging? Chugging?

ABNER: Trucking.

AMANDA: We were trucking along, nose to the grindstone. We were doing what was at our hand to do. An opportunity would come up; we'd say yes, and go for it. And then you came along. So, what was your plan? Did you have a plan back then? Because, it felt like it just got set into a groove, and all of a sudden, things were moving. Like, the chains on the bike got back on the wheel, and all of a sudden we were going somewhere versus just spinning our wheels. At what point did you think, *I know the way to do this,* or did it just happen over time? Because, I feel like you're the plan man. When I think of Jay King, I think of your notebook open with a billion notes in your perfect handwriting. And every day there are ideas and thoughts and plans and execution and who's gonna do it and how it's gonna happen. I have none of that. I just have to show up. Like, where do I go this year? You'll tell us. Going back to the mountaintop idea, it's like you joined us, strapped the backpack on with us, and we took a big leap.

185

ABNER: How'd that happen?

JAY: Well, I think the leap was that we found each other. I don't ever sit back and think, *I did this and I did that.* We found each other. Like, yo, you guys rescued me. You know what I mean? Despite everything that I had been working for and toward, there was always a missing thing. I was like, I've got to adjust my life because I want to find this. When we found each other, we agreed: *There's the mountaintop. We don't have it all planned out.* You have something that I don't have, and I have something that you guys don't have. But when you combine it together, it's like—

AMANDA: It's like that show where they drop you off in the wilderness with a stranger and you're allowed to bring one helpful item.

ABNER: Oh, yeah. *Naked and Afraid.* Or *Alive* or something.

JAY: Or *Alone,* or whatever it is. Oh, yeah. That's what it felt like. I even get chills talking about it. I know people say you need to sign that deal, you need to do this and that, give everything away to have one radio hit. I think, for me, that was the opposite of what I was looking for. You as a band were looking for the opposite of somebody pushing you to get a big

radio hit. I think of those backpacks being strapped on. We are both certain: We want legacy. We want to continue on, and the mountaintop never ends. I honestly don't see the top of the mountain. I hope the mountain is when they lay me in the casket, and that's the legacy for my kids.

ABNER: Wow.

JAY: Once we came together, my plan was like, *Okay, I'm on board. I'm going to give this 110 percent. And that's all I'm going to think about.* I wasn't thinking about building a company. This was not it. That's what's crazy. I wasn't thinking of creating the Jay King company, then finding artists. Remember, Abner? I asked if you guys wanted to partner up on a management company together. I wasn't looking to start anything. I just wanted to be invested in the band. And that's all I did. I thought, *I'm just going to go until the wheels fall off and we'll see what happens.* Looking back now, I think the plan really was to find other people like us, other people who would put their backpacks on, too. Who are those other people? We trusted each other to filter through them. I remember getting back to Nashville, and you texting me saying, "Yo, there's a guy you need to go meet." You guys were doing *Smokey Joe's Café.*

ABNER: We were doing a musical. Back then we would say yes to everything. A friend of ours was a Broadway actor and began this nonprofit theater program in Franklin, Tennessee, called Studio Tenn. Studio Tenn was doing *Smokey Joe's Cafe,* which was like a jukebox musical. We said yes to the musical. Amanda and I were back in Nashville for it, and we had just finished the Sunday matinee with another show scheduled that night. My mom had flown up to see us. I remember this big, good-looking, older white man from South Carolina who came up to me. "You Abner?" he asked. I said, "Yes, sir." He said he wanted to talk to me, that he was a booking agent and had heard a lot about Amanda and me. But while he was talking to me, I saw a guy across the room who used to be at—

AMANDA: —Motown.

ABNER: Yeah, he was the old president of Motown Records. And I was hanging in the lobby just because I wanted to meet him. Maybe he had a hookup. Maybe he was my eagle who was going to swoop us up to the mountaintop. So, I kind of brushed off this man talking to me and went to the Motown guy. I introduced myself, and he said he knew me. Then he said, "Do you know who you were just talking to?" I told the Motown guy I couldn't remember the man's name. "That was Bobby Cudd. And whatever

he says to you, you better listen." That's the best advice I've ever had. I was like, "Okay," then just ran out the door. I ran, and saw Bobby standing on the sidewalk waiting on his car to come. I said, "Bobby, I'm so sorry. Is there a chance we can grab a drink? I gotta get back in there for the second show today, but I'd love to get a drink, whatever." He agreed, so Bobby Cudd and I met for ten minutes. It was all the time I could give him because Mom was waiting. I went back to Amanda, in the dressing room, and said, "Amanda, I know I am prone to exaggeration. I know I get pie-in-the-sky sometimes. But I think I just met our guy. I really think I just met our guy." And I remember expecting her to roll her eyes at me, but she absolutely didn't. She said, "All right, well, let's introduce him to Jay." And I remember getting the call from Jay after he had met with Bobby. And Jay was like, "Man, I just met with Bobby, I think I just met our guy." *[Laughter.]*

AMANDA: Bobby said, "You know, I want to be on the horse when it gets to buckin'."

ABNER: That's right. I love that saying.

AMANDA: He was like, "You know, I really love you guys. I've been hearing about you. It's the first time I've gotten to see you. And I would love to work with you."

ABNER: And we're like, "We don't have a label. We don't have anything else." Oftentimes booking agents don't wanna work with you unless you have a label. And labels don't really want to work with you unless you've got a booking agent. It's the dog chasing its tail. Everybody waiting for somebody else to make the first jump before they actually act. But Bobby was like Jay, jumping in with nothing else. Like, *All right, I love this. This one, I'm part of. Let's go.* And I remember we asked him what he saw in us and why he would take such a big leap, signing us as an act. Bobby said, "Abner, I want you to know, I want to be on the horse when it

gets to buckin', 'cause if I'm not, I don't deserve to be on it in the first place."

JAY: My whole thought was, *The world has got to hear JOHNNYSWIM. Period.* You talk about big strategy. The strategy was—

AMANDA: The world's got to hear.

JAY: This is amazing. And I love it. So, the strategy was, *How does the world get to hear this? I don't know how we do it, but we're going to do it.* I remember when you guys were doing *Smokey Joe's Café,* and there was so much disconnect. I believed right away you had to start branding JOHNNYSWIM. And I learned early on, JOHNNYSWIM is always in all capital letters. Also, don't ask them to do a Donna Summer cover. That does not go, because I made that mistake, honestly. Remember, I was like, "The world's got to hear it. Let's just do this." And then Abner's like, "Eh. No." And I said, "Cool." [*Laughter.*] From that point on, when you told me to meet up with Bobby, I met up with Bobby. You can just see it, right? You can just see the people who had already shed their skin. I don't know any way else to say it, but it's like everybody we have connected with—the bullshit is gone. The skin is gone. You know and I know when we meet somebody, we don't care what name is on your business card. We don't care about—

ABNER: Your résumé or your huge brownstone on Central Park West.

JAY: Or what your office looks like. I don't even care who you worked with in the past. That's the thing. Bobby was working with country legends, but that had nothing to do with where we were headed. And he was willing to raise his hand and leverage it all. I remember that, personally. I felt like I had to get this out to the world. What were we going to do? And Bobby's response: "We're going to play. We're going to play. That's going to be the thing that we do." And we would show up almost every Saturday. Me and him and his map, in his backyard. He printed out this big map of the United States. I still have it to this day. I think it's in my closet. I kept one of them.

ABNER: If you ever took a picture, I want to put that in the book.

JAY: I don't know where he got it from, but he had this big picture of the United States. It was like a poster board. We put it on his back porch and then said, "Okay, what city do we think we can possibly own?" We knew New York, Nashville, L.A., were our spots. But we started to ask, "What do you think about this place?" We would smoke cigars, have a whiskey, and we would old-school-route in our minds. Bobby would say he knew

somebody who might give us a chance, at some theater, in some town. One of the first things we did was with—who was that band?

ABNER: Old Crow Medicine Show. One of my favorite tours ever. It was amazing.

JAY: That was one of those things where he leveraged everything. It didn't matter. He called. He would pick up and say, "Yo, you got it."

ABNER: For people to get the picture, understand Bobby has been in the business for such a long time. He's got people. He calls them and says, "Trust me." There are people who listen to Bobby Cudd when he says, "Trust me." Because Bobby Cudd doesn't do that for everybody. I remember the night we went to dinner in New York City when we were going to sign with Bobby. We were going to sign with Paradigm, and be an official part of the team. Bobby was going to be our booking agent. I remember, as a joke, I walked out and said, "Bobby, we don't really like to sign stuff. We do blood pacts. We cut our hands and shake on it." And I remember he said, "Where's the knife?"

JAY: I do remember that. I think we were at that French restaurant.

ABNER: Yeah. It's not there anymore. Bourdain's old spot, Les Halles. I feel like, when people imagine gathering the right team, they imagine something like *The Avengers. This* is how you make the team that makes a legendary career in music. Maybe that is for some people, but it's not for us. I think what everybody imagines when they look at building a career in music is that you have to add your booking agent and your label, and it's like adding superheroes. Everybody's got otherworldly talents, and it's instantly stratospheric. But no. It's *Mad Max,* man. You've got a guy who giggles weird who just fixed that tire for you playing lead guitar while that house is burning down. It's ugly, it's dirty, it's gritty. And it's more beautiful than the neat and clean thing I had dreamt of could ever be. Because here you had Bobby Cudd, who's had decades of work in the industry—blood, sweat, and tears into it, built a thing—leveraging all of it for us. He put us on the main stage because of his relationships. He put us on the main stage at New Orleans Jazz Fest when we had no reason to be the direct support for the Alabama Shakes, playing in front of twelve thousand people.

AMANDA: I think it was more than twelve thousand.

ABNER: Oh, right. It was like thirty or forty thousand people. And there was no reason for us to be there. We shouldn't have been on stage in front of forty thousand people that day. To this day, it's one of my top three musical experiences of all time. We got on stage, and nobody was paying attention. Everybody, including Bobby, said, "Don't start with a slow song. . . ." So we started with a slow song (that's legit JOHNNYSWIM 101. Telling us not to do a thing that we want to do is basically daring us to try it). Immediately, a few people in the front stopped talking and started watching. By the end of the set, we had all thirty thousand people engaged, all thirty thousand people watching. And I remember us just setting down our instruments. Because we didn't have a crew that was going to come clean our instruments; we would wave, we'd bow, we'd walk backstage, and then when the crowd started talking, we'd come back out ourselves and collect our instruments and put them in the cases, then go and put them in the van and drive to the next city. I remember it was me and Amanda, obviously, Drew Taubenfeld playing guitar. Markus Huber was playing bass. Rico Allen was playing drums. At this Jazz Fest, we put our instruments down, we waved, we bowed, we walked behind the stage, and we all hugged and sobbed like babies.

AMANDA: Actually, I think there's a picture somewhere of the two of us.

ABNER: If there's a picture, we need to find it so bad. We just hugged and cried because we knew—*we knew*—that was once in a lifetime. And that experience wouldn't have happened without somebody like Bobby Cudd putting his *Mad Max* face on and being like, "I don't care what you say . . ."

JAY: " . . . You gotta trust me."

ABNER: Leveraging all his relationships, all his credibility. *Trust me.*

JAY: To your credit, I will say this, hands down. I will say that in our strategy, there was only one real strategy. It was this: *We've got to put them in front of as many people as we've got.* That was really it. Because to me, there's something about an artist that everybody says about them, "You gotta check this out." There's something about the fact that I had so much confidence, probably too much confidence. Not that I was cocky, but I was like, *Listen, I'll put these mother******s up in front of anybody, anybody, I'm telling you right now.* I had that kind of confidence. I've never had that. Maybe with one or two artists, but I didn't manage them. The strategy was to get JOHNNYSWIM in front of anybody, and they're going to do their shit.

ABNER: Jay, my mom is gonna read this; cuss less.

JAY: Yeah, sorry. The awesome thing about that, though, is: You do it. There is never a time that you don't deliver. For instance, I might say, "Yo, we're in an office and you're going to sing." And you guys kill it. The ego is not there. There's never been a time where you were like, *I'm too good for that.* Or *I've already done that.* There's not one other artist I've ever worked with who's had that same say-yes attitude.

ABNER: The only thing we say no to is when Amanda turns something down because it's too late. *[Laughter.]* There was that South by Southwest one-thirty-in-the-morning set.

AMANDA: I did do that.

JAY: You did do it. Yes.

ABNER: Yes, the first time, you did.

AMANDA: Then the next time we had to take a red-eye, do a show, then take a red-eye back and go on tour, I said, "Hard pass. Jay—you can wear the wig."

JAY: Yes, there are definitely nos. And the nos should grow more now. But I would say, though, there was this energy, early on, where I felt, I don't know, I felt like a proud father. *Yeah, my kid's better than yours.* I wanted to open up. I wanted any spot that you would give me. I remember I would stay up to one, two o'clock in the morning. And every place that I could find to email, I would email. I've always felt like I could put you guys in any situation, and you would just nail it.

ABNER: That thing has never changed. It's like what you said, Jay. You put it perfectly. "I don't see the mountaintop; I think it's just a steady incline. At some point it'll be the mountaintop when you put me in my casket and I've left a legacy for my children and their children." I think that's exactly right, because for us, we got a book, we've got some TV shows coming out.

JAY: We've got a new album.

ABNER: We've got people who show up for shows. We've got a great life and a solid touring life and a great career. But we haven't settled. Nothing's changed. It's funny. When we have moments like these where we sit back and we get to reminisce, it's only in looking back that we really see how far we've come, you know what I mean? And it's that old picture. You know that old poster they'd have up in church, growing up. It's a couple sets of footprints in the sand. Jesus is saying in the poster, "When you see the two sets of footsteps, that's when I was walking next to you."

AMANDA: "And when you see only one set . . . that's when I was carrying you."

ABNER: It's sort of like that with us three. No one is carrying anyone, but sometimes there are three sets of footsteps and occasionally a set of feet or two are being dragged across the sand a ways. Each of us taking turns helping the others to keep moving forward.

AMANDA: *[Laughs because Abner is so cute.]*

ABNER: I think what happened with us from the very beginning was that there is an alignment of our assignment. I'm sorry if it sounds like a sermon, but there was an alignment in our assignment early on that we all latched on to. We latched on, and we started that uphill climb. The climb itself is joyful. We take joy in the work, and so we get to look back. Oh, yeah, we did come a long way. We don't hang our hat on it, because the work is full of joy. And the three of us together— because, really, JOHNNYSWIM is Amanda, Abner, and Jay King—we take such joy in it. Yes, there are landmarks. We want to see those little goals we want ahead of us. We want this book to sell well. We want people to watch the TV show and love it. We want to sell more tickets next year than we've ever sold.

AMANDA: I think we celebrate along the way.

ABNER: We absolutely celebrate.

JAY: Yeah, for sure.

ABNER: French fries and champagne along the way. As much as possible. But I think there's such a testament to finding the right people. When you do, you stop daydreaming about reaching the mountaintop and you start daydreaming about getting to work.

JAY: I just remember thinking, *I don't have an end point.* And that's very true. I tell this to other managers when they say, "How do you know when you've gotten to the place you want to go?" And I say, "You never do." Think about it. If I got to the place I want to go, then my job's over. *[Laughter.]*

AMANDA: I was thinking about my mom the other day. Something's really stuck with me since she passed. I would always be kind of upset because there were so many things she was working on. It wasn't like she was kind of cruising, like she was retired and just kind of enjoying life. She was working on shows. She was writing a musical. She loved designing. And she was coming out with a furniture line for outdoor furniture, which she was super passionate about. It was something she never got to do. She loved painting, and she always had dreams. There was never a time she didn't have dreams. So, when she passed away, it always felt unfair. I always felt like, *Well, crap. God, you took her too early. She still had so much to do.* And, literally, just a day or two ago, I looked at Abner and said, "I finally get it." I thank God she showed me something: I want to die with dreams. I can't imagine getting to a point in my life where I am just, *Okay, cool,* and that's it. Maybe when I'm a hundred. But I think when I'm a hundred and I've got a bunch of grandkids, I'll be like—

JAY: You'll have another thing.

AMANDA: I hope I die with dreams. And I feel like that's the one thing where we're all on the same page.

JAY: That's it. And we're willing to support each other in that journey.

ABNER: I wanna make sure we say this. We're so happy. Bobby Cudd was our first booking agent. He's not our booking agent anymore, but we're so honored to have worked with Bobby. We're so lucky to be with Marty Diamond and Ash Lewis. They have also greatly changed our lives, as our booking agents.

JAY: They have the same spirit.

ABNER: They have the same DNA, and they've got the biggest artists on the planet. But they are no less eager when they work with us, and we're so grateful. Bobby is not there anymore, but the people who took that role have elevated us even more. And they've made just as many sacrifices. And, like you said, they've shed that skin as well. They're people we don't just talk about business with. They're people we can sit with and have a real conversation about life, about heartache, about hard things we're going through, and celebrate together. And that's why we've got a great team today.

JAY: I think that's because the three of us don't put down our backpacks.

ABNER: Right.

AMANDA: I want to make a toast: Cheers to dying with dreams.

MY GRANDPA'S MISSING FINGER

Amanda

WE HAVE TRIED TO KEEP THE meaning of the name JOHNNYSWIM a secret. But maybe we've gone too long without telling you the truth. So here goes. . . .

We know JOHNNYSWIM is not a microwave. Our career is an oven.

The phrase "a watched pot never boils" should have been my motto. It would have saved me some sleepless nights. Finally, it seemed the momentum was building. The meetings that had seemed to be fruitless wastes were beginning to flower. Songs were being heard and loved, and a team of champions assembled around us. It was pretty fun. Abner and I had been working out since the New Year and were feeling pretty dang hot. We were excited and expectant. This was going to be our year.

We were going by the name The Neon Orchard, something Abner came up with in his time at art school. Its meaning has escaped my memory, but even then, it barely made sense. It's sort of like how you keep your screen name you made when you first got on the Internet. I was so proud of my screen name: Shuggs14.

Shuggs was short for Sugar; I was a clever fourteen-year-old. I didn't realize how absurd it was until about three years ago, in my thirties.

"The Neon Orchard" was cool, but all these years later, it wasn't quite sticking. Not with our audiences, who still just called our band "Abner and Amanda."

Around this time, my grandfather got sick. Lou Sudano was a tall, sweet-talking, granddaughter-loving, honey-voiced Italian man from Brooklyn, with the best head of hair you've ever seen in your life. He lived with us when I was little on our ranch in Thousand Oaks, California, and I spent most of my days after school following him around and getting in his way. I would set a wineglass for him at his place at the table every night at dinner, and in return, every Saturday morning Grandpa Lou would make me pancakes with his special ingredient, a little squirt of maple syrup. He was charming and kind and stubborn and smart, and very, very dear to me.

We knew the end was coming. He was in his eighties and had fearlessly smoked a pack a day for as long as I could remember. When the cancer came, he made no attempt to fight it, and we made little attempt to change his mind. He was old and tired and wanted to enjoy the time he had left. We couldn't fault him for it.

A month or so before he passed, we visited him at my grandmother's house in New Jersey. They had divorced in the seventies or eighties, but they still lived down the street from each other and saw each other almost daily. She would cook his dinner, he would fix her house, and they'd both ignore how much they acted like they were still married. But there was less fighting with their less-binding relationship. At his funeral, the waitress from his favorite restaurant came and she asked for my grandma Margaret. She told my grandma that every time she had asked Lou why he was single, he shook his head and said, "There was only ever one woman for me, and I married her." My grandmother wept when she heard this, and so did all of us grandkids.

On that day near the end of Grandpa Lou's life, we arrived at my grandmother's house ready to be sad. The tests didn't look good, and we assumed he wouldn't look good, either, but to our surprise he was in great shape and full of life, his hair still thick and his muscles strong. I hugged him tightly and allowed myself the rest of the day to ignore the truth that I'd be losing him soon. Ignorance in the face of death is bliss.

We ate Grandma's classic Italian food (the smell of tomatoes and basil can still make me feel like a kid again);

my grandpa sang songs in his resounding tenor; my dad let his mother pamper him; my mom told bad jokes; and my sisters and I rolled our eyes. The day was perfect. After a few lovely hours, we peeled our suctioned skin from the plastic furniture covers that protected my grandma's pink-and-gold antique sofa and made our way to the car.

As we walked to the front door down the old hallway lined with sepia-toned pictures of all my grandmother's dearly beloved siblings, I held Grandpa Lou's hand for what I didn't realize would be the last time. My fingers traced his big palms and caught on the shortened end of his right pointer finger. It had been deformed and misshapen as long as I could remember, but he had never told me the true story of how it happened. Sometimes he said it was an accident at the factory he used to work at. Sometimes he used it as a cautionary tale to warn us of the dangers of using sharp scissors. And sometimes he said my grandma bit him when she was mad. All lies. But I loved them.

Lies can be fun.

We left my grandmother's house and drove in silence to the highway, each of us in our own way trying to burn the day into our memory. Finally, after twenty-eight years, I asked my dad for the truth. How did Grandpa lose that bit of finger?

It was a simple story. During the war, a boat capsized off the coast of France, where he was stationed. In an attempt to rescue the passengers, my grandfather released the rope tying the rescue boat to the dock, and his finger got stuck in the quick untangling of the cord. As the rest of the guys frantically tried to release my grandfather's finger, his friend Johnny dove right in and swam to the boat with a float. "Swim, Johnny, swim!" the growing number of onlookers shouted. And one by one, Johnny, swimming back and forth, saved each of the six soldiers who had been on the small, defunct boat.

They tried to give my grandfather a Purple Heart to commemorate his injury in service, but he wouldn't accept it. My father was proud of any award given to his father, and tried to convince him to take it. Grandpa said stoically, "If people remember anything, I hope it's not my stupid finger being cut off. I hope they remember the hero. I hope they remember Johnny and how he swam."

From that day on, we were no longer The Neon Orchard. In memory of my grandfather, his friend, and his finger, we would be called JOHNNYSWIM, then and always.

Abner

WE ARE RIVERS, NOT LAKES.

Not sure where we heard this first, but it's been a mantra in our marriage and individual lives for years. The basic idea is that a lake, having no inlet or outlet, has a limited supply of resources and, therefore, a limited amount of life in it. A river, however, flourishes as it moves from one place to another, in constant motion. Always creating new life. Always giving and receiving. Never concerned that the supply will run out. We try to take that approach to our time, to our money, and especially to our creative endeavors. We're not worried about the well drying up any more than a river is concerned with getting more water to flow through it.

I am not and never really have been worried that my best song is behind me. Who's to say what the "best song" is anyway?! Is it the song a young man heard on his drive to jump off a bridge that caused him to pause for just long enough to change his mind and commit to taking one more breath than he had planned? Or is it the song that made the most money? Or is it the song that reignited a romance that helped two people stay on the course toward a healed marriage? Or is it the song that my Uber driver might recognize if I hummed him the chorus?

My actual fear is that I would ever *begin* to worry that our best song is behind us. Because it would be the greatest evidence that something is different in *me,* not in our songwriting. The work is too important for commercial measurements of success to take the driver's seat. It would be like worrying that I might forget how to have a conversation. The point of conversation isn't to have the best talk you've ever had, but to communicate. We don't write to get out a better song than anyone else. We write because something is alive in us and it must come out. Comparison is the thief of joy and a freaking dream killer.

We are rivers, not lakes.

Michelangelo famously said: "In every block of marble I see a statue as plain as though it stood before me, shaped and perfect in attitude and action. I have only to hew away the rough walls that imprison the lovely apparition to reveal it to the other eyes as mine see it." I find that the more Amanda and I write, the less time we spend forcing the song out and the more time we spend waiting for the song to come to us. I don't know if that's a sign of mature songwriting or laziness, honestly. But Amanda and I always hope we will hear the song before we ever write it—in a sense, *receiving* it rather than conjuring it into existence. It feels like the grown, mature way of doing things.

All that being said, songwriting can be so dang boring sometimes. The writing of "Home" (the song that basically bought us our house) was neither mature nor patient nor seen ahead of time nor "received" nor revealed as a beautiful apparition, nor any of the eloquent things I could write about the act of songwriting. Instead, it was a complete mess born out of frustration.

When we sit to write a song, I expect it to tear through my chest, unhinged and wild. I expect to worry about getting all the brilliance that's spilling out of me down on paper while I can still grasp it. I expect triumph. I expect tears. I expect angelic visitation or a glory cloud or something. Then I blink, and find I've just been sitting there for an hour daydreaming and accomplishing zilch. It was on one such day when Amanda and I sat with our longtime collaborator, Britten Newbill (Hendersonville, Tennessee's greatest), in hopes of penning a three-and-a-half-minute aria that would be beloved and bellowed from mountaintops for as long as humans have lungs. Boy, did we write a ton of trash that day. We woooorked to make something awesome, and all we came away with was a lot of trying. Hours of it. Hours of trying don't keep the lights on. And at that point in our marriage, having our lights turned off was a very real fear. We didn't really

have any furniture in our new apartment in L.A., other than a bed and a place to fold and place old T-shirts. The landlord had a couple of outdoor chairs we brought into the apartment for this session. We snacked like crazy on some almonds and wrote all day. We wanted so badly to write something great. But we really couldn't seem to make heads or tails of any rabbit hole we went down.

After what felt like a week of bad songwriting, we were ready to call it a day but instead opened a bottle of cheap wine. There we were, three deflated songwriters ready to forget the day.

Annoyed that we hadn't called down angelic legions with our stanzas, I was was happy to open Two-Buck Chuck, but I would be damned if we didn't write *something* that day. "I know we've been at this for eight hours," I said to Britten and Amanda, "but let's just finish something, *anything* in the next few minutes." I grabbed the guitar and started playing a simple folk groove, and chuckled to myself as I thought of an opening line that almost felt satirical: "Right round the corner, down by the canyon, I met a man who lost his way."

We laughed, and drank some cheap wine.

"He said, 'I'm Saul, born the son of a sailor, who never showed me his face.'"

More laughs.

More wine.

Was the wine really *that* bad?

"My daddy's gone, and my momma met her maker."

(Oof. In the years to come, this line was hard to sing. Do you instantly know when you've written something damningly prophetic, or do you only realize it in hindsight?)

Wine.

"Home."

Music.

"I need me some home."

Wine.

Well, *that* sure felt good to sing.

Music.

The song was done before the bottle was.

Took us twenty minutes of "joking around." Pouring cheap wine and pouring our hearts out by accident—not a bad day for some impoverished songwriters. Who knew that night would change everything?

We went on to record the song by spending our last two hundred dollars on a microphone and borrowing a software disk from Amanda's dad, Bruce (aka Brucie, aka Grandpa, aka Peepa).

I didn't know how to record. I had to call a friend and ask how to start recording. "Just press the letter R, dude."

Oh, okay, cool cool cool, we've got this.

That day, we made the recording that's out now. With the same two-hundred-dollar mic you hear on the theme song for *Fixer Upper.* The same super-amateur harmonica playing. Just some kids slinging wine and chasing dreams. Not overly worried about how we were gonna keep the lights on. Just trying to do the next right thing.

The song came from someplace, but who knows where? It's kind of three different stories that all end up talking about needing "home." I'm still not sure where the stories came from, and I wouldn't know how to find them again if I tried. I'm glad we did it then, because the journey may only ever have been offered that one time.

How will the next song happen? I don't know. But I'm not real worried about it.

We are rivers, not lakes.

Creativity is a wild, wild thing. I, personally, don't believe that any one person is more or less creative than another. I believe creativity exists outside us. It's a well from which everyone can partake as often as they like. Some just know the way to it better than others. And some have more tools, or ones they're more used to, that allow them to mold what they come away with into something they can display.

Creativity doesn't belong to anyone any more than genius does. I believe we are visited by genius (and hope it finds us at work). And I believe we all have the privilege to visit that well of creativity. It is the very same well that was drawn upon to sing the universe into existence. Man, what I wouldn't give to hear that song, to feel the frequencies of that melody as it flung stars into life. Whole worlds and their inhabitants, their stories, their dramas and comedies coming into being. The uprisings of the workers, the luxuries of the rich, the beasts of the deep, the beasts of the air, the triumphs and tragedies of millennia times millennia times millennia all scattered through space and time, via the conscious vibration of a Voice.

Just as I believe that same Spirit that raised Jesus from the grave is alive in me and can work unspeakable power, so I also believe the Source of creativity, from which all that we know came to be, is available to everyone and is capable of working immeasurable beauty.

Hey, the pressure is off of "being creative." The pressure is on how often you'd like to make your withdrawal from the well.

So remember . . . and I'm counting you in on this, as well. . . .

We are rivers, not lakes.

WE ARE RIVERS, NOT LAKES.

Amanda

CREATIVITY AND CHILDBIRTH have a lot in common. There is pain in the process and fear in the formation. New creations always come at a cost. The key, I've learned, is not to force something to life, but rather learn to let go.

I gave birth to all my beautiful babies at home. Some of you will read that and think, *Oh wow, that's awesome!* Others, probably a larger portion of you, might feel just a tad bit of terror rising up in you. Maybe you're wondering about the safety of home birth or you think I'm a hippie or some sort of moon-worshipping witch now. Or maybe you're horrified because, yes, having a baby at home means—you guessed it—no pain medication.

Fear not, I am neither a hippie nor a witch, and my births were all safe and lovely. As it turns out, they came on too fast for me to have gotten to the hospital anyway (Luna holds the record for the fastest birth in the house, at a speedy thirty-four minutes). But, unfortunately, you'd be right about the pain meds. The midwife shows up at your house with equipment that's the equivalent of a level-1 hospital's, but there is nary an anesthesiologist in sight. It's the price you pay for getting to eat whatever you want and not having strangers stare at your privates during labor. Seemed fair to me.

So with all my babies, I chose the menu: French fries for Joaquin, Raisin Bran for Luna, and passion fruit ice cream for Paloma. I also chose the guest list: Abner; my sisters; my bestie, Tessa; and our midwives. Beyond that, I chose very little. My births were natural in every sense. I couldn't choose the date or the time. I couldn't choose the pace or the pressure. There were no real interventions, no slowing things down, no speeding things up, nothing to make it easier except for taking a warm bath and getting a back rub. I'll admit back rubs are really nice, but by no means do they numb what my birthing books saccharinely call "waves of discomfort." All I could do was let my primal brain take over and let my body do what women have always done to birth the next generation.

I had been to a few births and watched more documentaries on them than an ob-gyn, but really, I had no clue. I assumed childbirth was mostly pushing, and that my sheer will would force the baby out. Well, I was wrong. A solid 90 percent of birthing a human is about relaxing. Just floating off in your brain and getting out of your body's way. Then, when it's time to push, don't worry, your body will do

that for you. Buckle up and enjoy the ride.

I would say giving birth is unlike anything else in the world, but the more babies I have, the more I realize how much of life and art are in it. So often the best things in life and art come when we free ourselves from our own mental seatbelts, dip into our most primal places, and let go. That's not to say it's not work. Sometimes relaxing is harder work than striving. Rest is a weapon, one that takes practice to wield.

The best songs I've written, or at least started writing, came from these instinctive places. They may not be the most poppy songs we have, or the most popular, but they are the songs I hope my kids will cherish one day, because they are the most truthful ones, the ones I felt most vulnerable writing. "Georgica Pond" is one of those. That song didn't come by force. It came by surrender. Creativity, like giving birth, and even like praying, is listening more than it is speaking. And that song felt like it was sung to me before I ever sang it. The hope is that we allow ourselves to be the vessels we were intended to be, carrying and pouring out the things we were intended to carry and pour out. It seems like that should be easy, but it's not. I don't know why it's not, but it's not. The harder life gets, the harder it is to do.

When I was pregnant with Joaquin, I prayed for a pain-free birth. God said, "I love you so much, but no." I kept lobbing that prayer up just in case, but soon a different desire formed in me. Pain is one thing. Fear is another. If I was going to petition for something, it wouldn't be for no pain, it would be for no fear. So I prayed for a fear-free birth, and God said, "Let's do this."

That said, let me tell you about *transition*. Transition is the very last and very hardest part of giving birth. If you've ever seen a woman on TV giving birth, screaming, cussing, damning people, what you were seeing was a woman in transition. I was told I would know I was in transition when I started feeling like I couldn't do it anymore, when I wanted to give up. You know what? They were right. Each baby, minutes before joining us, probably heard me crying, "I'm done! I need a break!" Transition is the hardest phase, but it's by far the shortest one, and it comes right before the relief and a new life arrive. I believe it's the same with creativity and life in general. They're often hardest right before something new comes.

So, instead of requesting ease, let's ask for fearlessness, and do our work in the freedom that comes with it. Let's trust our way into the process, just like we might approach giving birth. And then, when it gets too hard, let's know we're too close to give up, and trust our way out.

Amanda

TRAVELING WITH KIDS IS NOT FOR
the faint of heart. It will tax every muscle
you have, from your biceps all the way
down to your patience—which scientifically
is the second most used muscle in parent-
hood. Right behind love, obviously. You
pack more things, unpack more things, forget more things, buy more things, lose more
things, repeat more things, yell more things,
whisper-scream more things, and may even
need to employ a leash at some point. There
is no judgment. Kids on the road is a lawless
place. It is wild and exhausting.

But let me tell you. It's wonderful.

We found our rhythm soon after
Joaquin was born, but it took a minute.
At six weeks old, he was turning into
quite the yummy cupcake of a baby, with
big gooey lips dripping with more joyful
giggles than a heart could even handle.
He was about as easy a baby as can be.
But, you know, newborns aren't known
for their ease of care. Believe it or not, it
thrilled me to head out on tour. I wanted
to get back to things as usual. I missed the
road. I missed the sense of purpose I felt
there. I missed our people. I missed seeing
new cities and old friends. I felt lost in
this new world of schedules, a thing I
knew little to nothing about before Joaquin
came along. And I looked forward to

gaining some confidence back by bringing him into a world I knew so well.

There're just so many things people don't tell you about living with babies, and the learning curve is so steep. For example, I didn't realize all my wardrobe choices would change post-baby, because it never dawned on me how often I would need to use my boobs. Our poor band and crew got locked out of a lot of green rooms due to my forgetting to dress appropriately to pump and nurse.

"Sorry, guys. Mama wore a turtleneck maxi dress and needs to get 97 percent naked for the next twenty minutes or so. Don't have too much fun without me."

I did a lot of "research," aka panic googling, but still had only a fraction of a clue when we first set out post-baby.

In my defense, there was no reference guide for touring with babies. We had to play it loose and fast and be willing to grow and learn and give ourselves lots of grace. It was a crash course. After one

show in Chicago when Joaquin was a few months old, we flew at 5:00 A.M. (that's 3:00 A.M. for our West Coast baby) to a private college event in Ohio. The information for the event was fairly muddled by the time it funneled down to me, so as we pulled up, I realized in horror that the event was taking place entirely outside in the summer heat. No dressing room, no indoor bathroom, just a tent for everyone to share, with some plastic bottles of warm water stacked on a folding table. There was exactly one folding chair. A car dropped us off with all our gear and drove away, taking our only chance of air-conditioning with it.

My sweet baby, exhausted from the journey and the middle-of-the-night wake-up call, was inconsolable. I tried wearing him in a wrap, rocking him, strolling him, but on top of the heat, the blaring music from the stage made a good nap nearly impossible. Finally, before running onstage for our set, I opened his

Pack 'n Play under a tree as far (but not *too* far) from the stage as I could find. I nursed him in the breeze, set him down in the shade, and my dear friend Connie stayed with him until he cried himself to sleep.

There is a picture of this somewhere on my Instagram. It looks sweet. It wasn't. It was a rough day, to say the least. I felt ill-prepared and ill-equipped. But I learned something. I learned that sometimes you have to walk out the worst-case scenario to the finish to realize you're going to be okay.

We've had a lot of weird days like that since, where none of the plans worked out, the flights got canceled, the hotels had no rooms, the shows went too late, and we booked flights that were too early. After three babies and five years, those are the kinds of days I've come to welcome, hesitantly but graciously. They keep me sharp and flexible and remind me of what I want for these little blessings I get to call mine. That they would, quicker than we did, learn the joy in bending before they break.

There's a holy discomfort in being away from home. Your eyes are twice as wide and your ears are twice as open. Your inner cruise control is disabled, at least for a bit. It's a magic that can only really happen when you leave your house and go live outside your norm. Being comfortable in discomfort is a hard-earned gift, but its value is exponential.

Sure, that day in Ohio was a nightmare, but since then, in moments where everything seems to be going wrong, I can look back and say, *Oh look, that turned out just fine, we made it through, and everyone ended the day happy and healthy.* We were together, and we made that little valley of discomfort home. What a gift, what a treasure. Just like in birth or in yoga, you breathe through the tight spots, and nothing gets broken.

One day, these kids of ours won't be ours to keep anymore. That's the way it should be. We raise them up to send them out. My hope is that when it's their turn, they won't shy away from discomfort or the unknown. That when adventures and opportunity call from beyond the horizon of their status quo, they won't be afraid to sail toward those new experiences.

I love taking my kids with me, despite the fatigue of my body, heart, and mind some days, because one day, if we do it right, they'll be teaching us how to love better, listen better, and live better. Without the shackles of fear, they'll have the world within their grasp. One day they'll be holding my hand and walking me out into some unknown. One day, my ceiling will, I hope, be their floor. But first we have to be okay with a few outdoor naps, inconsolable babies, and missed flights.

Abner

IF IT CAME DOWN TO IT AND I had to pick only one thing I could do for the rest of my professional life, my choice would take no time. I would choose performing. The person onstage sets the tone for what happens in the room. When we step onstage, we hope you're entertained, but our hearts, our intentions, and our prayers are for more to happen.

As Amanda's dad says, "If it's not alive, it's not live." In some weird way, being onstage is like meditation. Throughout the day, I constantly hear the buzz around me: the lists in my head of things to do and things forgotten and things I'm avoiding, whether consciously or subconsciously. But onstage, everything goes quiet and all the colors become more saturated. A mix of adrenaline and nerves and fear cause all of my and Amanda's senses to be hyperfocused for those ninety minutes. Not just on the music we're playing but on each other, on the band, and on the looks we're always sharing. Amanda and I literally have full conversations during songs, spoken solely through our faces and eyes. We could be talking about the drunk person in the balcony making a fool of himself, the joke we were telling just before getting onstage, or the fact that on this particular night I don't

DRUNKS

221

think I'm gonna hit that high note on the bridge coming up and I need her to cover for me. That's all happening while we're singing lyrics and leading the band.

But our most important job of the night is making room for you.

We don't just want to sing *in* cities, we want to sing *for* cities. We aren't onstage just so we can sing *to* you, we want to be there *with* you. That night is the only night in all of history like it. We'll never be together again on a night exactly like that one. The worries, concerns, joys, and victories that we all walk in with are singular in space and time. Never before or again in the vast cosmos does this night exist. The majority of our energy on any given night is always assigned to paying attention. Yes, to what's happening onstage but, more important, to what's happening in the room at large. I find it possible to give that attention in front of five people or fifteen thousand people. Just like a surfer rides one wave on a vast ocean, you can sense the swell of a large room and the direction we're all going in. You can lean into it, steer it, or pull the breaks. And not just for show. When we're all together in that room, this experience is a living thing—the sweat, the laughs, the tears—a thing greater than the sum of its parts.

DRUNKS

I can't imagine being one of those bands that just gets up onstage and sings the same set every night, judging how good the show was merely by how loud the crowd sang or even how flawless the musical performance was. Listen, we are not pop starlets. We didn't have one huge song that propelled us into the life of working musicians. This was and is a *grind.* If we've gotten anywhere, it's because we pay attention in every room at every phase. From the four-hour set at the wine bar where we play while people are eating dinner and not paying attention, to the sold-out Ryman Auditorium nights and beyond. We don't have the luxury of playing "that one song" to light up the night. We are your flight attendants and your pilot. We set the stage to be ready for takeoff and hope to catch air every night. And we don't always soar! That's the best part! It's *a living thing.* (Did I say that already? Am I mixing metaphors?)

We want to feel the sorrow you bring with you and we want to be able to feel that moment when you catch your breath and it finally falls off you. We believe you can come to a JOHNNYSWIM show walking with a limp and leave walking straight. We believe that when we all gather together, it is absolutely spiritual. You don't even have to believe the things

223

we believe. When we get together, we know something will move in the spirit realm, if we'll only make room for it. That's what we're believing for. We believe you can walk in lost, ready to give up on life, and leave with the fire of a thousand suns burning in your chest, excited to greet tomorrow boldly while you look your fears in the eye. We believe you can have had the worst argument ever in the car with the one you love, unearthing hard things you feel you may never recover from, then spend some time together with all of us and leave having let go of the very weight you thought would drown you. Leave more in love, leave more committed.

There is power in walking in your purpose.

We believe this is ours: When we are onstage, we strive to make that room a space for communion (people gathered together for a cause greater than the individuals) and a space for miracles. It's not because our voices are so good or because we're anointed or special. But if some loud trumpet blast could tear down the walls of Jericho, then who are we to limit the power of some love songs?!

It's never been about just the music; it's always been about people. Amanda and I see what we do as a service. When you see us onstage or on TV, I hope you understand that you are looking at two people who believe in *you.* We believe you are a singular expression of the universe, who will never be replicated again in the history of all existence. You are the *one* opportunity God afforded Himself to express His very nature in a way that only creating *you* would suffice to show to the cosmos. We are dust that was animated by a song! By the vibration of a voice! We unleash the very power that created Heaven and Earth when we sing together.

We don't want you to just like our songs; we want you to walk away better because of what you encounter at a JOHNNYSWIM show. We believe in the power of community, the power of communion, the power of our collective voices and attention. So *know* that when you walk into a room for a JOHNNY-SWIM show, you are part of the equation. The night would not be the same if you weren't there. We believe that every person who walks in carries gifts and supernatural strengths that help not just themselves, but also the people around them.

We believe that if the world is an ocean, our voices can move the sea together.

Oh man, we'll never stop singing, because we'll never stop believing in you. *We don't just want to sing* in *cities, we want to sing* for *cities!* Lemme say it louder for the people in the back! We are not just here to entertain you. We are here because Heaven itself rises to attention when we gather!

We believe miracles can happen at a freaking bar if we're all there together. We hope to use our gifts in a show simply to make room for what is available because you are there. It's not about us. Because we are onstage, we get to set the intention and create space, but the rest happens because you are there. We aren't really even necessary. The most amazing meal in the world is only as good as the people you get to eat it with.

When I see Heaven, I see a club, top-shelf booze only. We all have a glass held high, and we're all singing at the top of our lungs, singing songs that haven't been written yet, singing songs that flow like a river, pulling apart space and time to sing melodies from the heart of all creation. When I see Heaven, I see you. I see us all together. And it's a hell of a time. I see Heaven every time we walk onstage and you are there. I can't say it enough: There is power in your presence.

Amanda always says to our kids, "Our words are strong like our muscles." But man, I wouldn't give our muscles that much credit, to be honest. When we tell someone they are beautiful, it's not just a compliment. It's a truth that can speak directly into their soul. When we sing together, we're not just throwing fluffy nice-

ties into the sky. We are stirring up and bringing to life things in the very souls of people.

I've heard artists talk about how "exciting" performing can be. I'd humbly propose that if all you've felt is "excitement," then maybe you're doing it wrong. We are after Heaven itself. Every night. Whiskey in hand. Hearts to Heaven. Lungs growling. Sweat flowing. *Let's freaking go!* This thing we get to experience together isn't rote or common or just another night of shows. This thing is *alive!*

We are JOHNNYSWIM. This is what we do. Home is where the heart is, and ours are wide open. And you are most certainly invited!

WE ARE
JOHNNYSWIM.
THIS IS WHAT WE DO.

Amanda

IN EARLY 2020, WE SLOWLY crawled out of the fog brought on by the birth of our third baby, Paloma, into a year we confidently christened "Our Busiest Year Ever." We held on tight to the sleepy, lazy, wild, newborn days, knowing what awaited us: A new tour was around the corner, and with it, lots of travel, big arenas full of people thrilled to see Lauren Daigle (but not before being forced to see us, too), a new record for Goodbye Road (our collaboration with Drew Holcomb and Penny & Sparrow), a TV show airing on the new Magnolia Network, lots of flights, wild adventures, and crazy new momentum. Oh, and a new book (*wink wink*). We thought we'd barely be at home. The impending pandemic said, "Ha ha ha ha ha."

At the beginning of the year, I had this dreamlike vision of a race car speeding down a track. The faster it went, the more deliberate and slow the driver became. This inspired the mantra Abner and I created for the year: *Slow down to go fast*. It seemed obvious at the time, but we hadn't the smallest clue what that mantra would truly mean. None of us knew what the year held in store for us.

We forged ahead with our plans as the year advanced, confident of our direction, ignorant of the future. As the tour with Lauren Daigle was taking off, our dear friend Drew Holcomb met us in Dallas to write for the project that would take up the last half of our year, "Goodbye Road." The songs we wrote spoke of imperfect loves and the need to live even when the world is ending, but our conversations outside of those songs spoke of something else. They echoed the drudgery and impracticality of road life with a family.

Drew and his wife, Ellie, tour much like we do, splitting time at home, juggling three beautiful babies and two vibrant careers. They have been our role models for how it's done since we first got pregnant with Joaquin. Actually, Ellie was one of the only touring mamas I knew, and the first to give me the advice and encouragement I fervently needed. She convinced me we could do it. And we did.

The Holcombs, like us, had spent years dreaming of touring, then touring incessantly and building audiences. Somewhere along the way, we have all created a whole life and career over miles of pavement and long stretches of stages. We're all living our dream. But as we hung out on the bus between meet-and-greets and sound checks, and while I fold-

'TIL WE GET BACK AGAIN

ed laundry backstage after nursing the baby, and as we ate another non-home-cooked dinner in catering, our conversations kept going back to one thing. Now that we've built our dream life on the road, how do we get off the road? Not forever, obviously, because we love it. But how do we make touring something we *get* to do and not *have* to do?

Maybe we were feeling something in the ether we couldn't articulate or make sense of. This longing for home in the middle of what was meant to be a wild year—maybe it was preparing us for what was coming.

The tour had just started when we were forced to pack up, rushing and frantic and insecure of our future, just hoping to catch a flight home from Des Moines, Iowa. Originally, we thought COVID-19 would only take us out for about six weeks. As I type this, it's been fourteen (and many more months as I now look over the final edit).

The flight home itself felt apocalyptic. The cabin was quiet, a silence broken only by a sharp cough here and there, which, of course, everyone took notice of now. Then the cabin would get even quieter, a bit of fear lingering like smoke in the air. As the days progressed, what had felt like a small risk and a slight inconvenience earlier in the week thudded down on our shoulders, bearing the weight of what it actually was: a complete overhaul of our lives. It was disorienting and sobering. Especially for us. Touring musicians' lives and livelihood depend almost solely on traveling to crowded, minimally ventilated rooms—only the most risky activity in a pandemic.

Now those rooms would have to wait, just like the rest of the country.

Strangely enough, any other year we wouldn't have been able to afford life without a calendar full of shows. But we had spent most of my pregnancy with Paloma filming a little TV show called *Home on the Road,* which would air on Chip and Joanna Gaineses' Magnolia Network. Cameras and a very amazing crew family followed us around to a few shows in the summer and fall of 2019 and asked us a lot of questions on our couch back at home.

A few years earlier, Chip had called Abner one day while Abner was in the parking lot at Whole Foods. They chatted about ideas for a potential show on a potential network. It all felt so right. There might be two people on this earth who are more talented, creative, and generous than Chip and Jo—and, of course, if there are, I'd like to meet and work with them—but as far as I know, such a couple

doesn't exist. A show with Chip and Jo is a dream come true. It was a ton of work adding filming to our normal schedule of singing, babies, and, for me, building babies, but man oh man, was it worth it.

Because here I am now, writing this chapter, fourteen weeks into a pandemic quarantine. The expectation of a six-week hiatus now seems laughable, but that longing for home that seemed laughable back then is now magically our normal. Instead of waking up in new cities every day, we wake up to the consistent alarm clock of babies asking for food. We ride our days out trying to piece together creative, discerning thoughts while being asked for screen time for the thousandth time and trying to explain to our kids that we still have work. *Work* has always meant Abner and me in front of a microphone. Now it's us sitting quietly in front of a computer. The kids probably think we're online-shopping all day. *Relax, kids, Mommy does that for only half the day.*

We have managed to accomplish a few great things during quarantine. We potty trained Luna. We sleep trained Paloma. I've almost mastered making sourdough, and Abner has become quite the handyman. You can find him every Saturday serving up serious dad vibes while power washing the driveway in knee-high socks. We even recorded a six-song record with strangers we met on Instagram. Instead of doing it privately in a fancy studio over the course of months, we finished each song in about thirteen hours live online in the corner of our guest room/office, with Lego surrounding our feet like landmines. (I've also learned during this time that the plural of *Lego* is, in fact, *Lego.*)

The wins look a little different these days, but this whole season, the uncertainty and sadness of it, while weighty and at times overwhelming, has also been wonderful. It's been a lesson relearned every day—sometimes hour by hour and minute by minute—to not carry blessings as burdens. We as a family have never had time like this together. Ever. With no tour, no school, no distractions, no parties, no expectations. We are together and at home. And in the most unlikely way, we are lucky enough to keep the lights on. The hiatus hasn't been easy, but it's been a blessing. The pace is slow, and unfortunately for those we work with, so are our responses to emails.

The busy years are still ahead of us. There will be, I'm sure, more concerts one day, long tours, travels, and flights, and the beautiful chaos we've learned to thrive on. It's all still out there in front of us. But when that day comes, we'll hopefully be able to run that race with a bit more grace and perspective and kindness than we had before. We will see the blessings of the fruit trees fertilized by the manure this year has been, and hopefully, one day soon, when these very words are being read on a printed page, the world will be a better version of what it once was.

Until then, we'll learn to rest in the uncertainty. We'll learn to push our roots deep into the rocky soil. Until then, we go slow to go fast.

THE OTHER ABNER & AMANDA

Abner

WE REALLY DON'T EVER TELL PEOPLE the actual meaning behind the name JOHNNYSWIM. But today . . . *today* . . . right here, right now . . . finally, here's the absolute truth. You've made it this far. You deserve the straightforward, honest, easy-to-digest explanation of our band name. Here it is.

What we experience as life is really just one strand in a web of infinite possibilities, with endless paths created as our choices expand the perceived reality in real time around us. Bound as we are to our view of this illusion called time, we become slaves to universal "truths" that are really just one of many options. For some of us, this actuality is clearer than it could possibly be to normal, everyday humans.

I have been a time traveler for as long as I can remember, so my grasp of the greater reality is broad and sturdy, like an oversized book (not quite a memoir and not quite a coffee table book, but you're fond of it anyway), the sort of book you set your coffee mug on in the morning.

But on the morning I discovered our band name, I realized something was very different.

Usually when I make a time jump, it's as easy as passing through a door. I start here and "now" and end wherever and whenever I've decided to go. Some of my recent jumps had this weird, short blur in them, like two doors at each end of a six-inch hallway. But with each subsequent jump, the hallway began to grow longer. Eventually, I no longer jumped from time and place to time and place. Instead, I jumped to the hallway and strolled through it to the exit point.

On this particular day, I was leaving an ultimate Frisbee game at the Toluca Lake Baseball park when I got curious about what this space must have been like three hundred years ago. I *focused,* and the world around me became engulfed in light as I arrived into the new hallway. I

began the stroll that I knew would end at a singular door, predictably leading me to the era of my choosing.

But this time was different. The air shook as I entered the hallway and stared down at the door, which was surrounded by a strange, eroded molding. I knew things had been getting weird, but this was on a whole new level. I told myself to ignore it and just continue my stroll through time and space.

So I opened the door.

I was back at the Toluca Lake Baseball park, exactly where I had left it. This had never happened before. I was summoning my *focus* to jump back to the hallway, when I saw myself. Not existentially, not out of body; I stood there a hundred yards away from myself, laughing next to a beautiful woman I couldn't really see. Her laugh felt familiar even from a distance. I was no longer traveling only

through time and space but also through the echo of choices long ago made and forgotten. I had reentered the web of reality, riding a different strand this time.

I was in a parallel existence.

The parallel-universe, way-too-cool Other-Abner and the hot girl had their laughs interrupted by a buzz. In sync, they looked at their phones, then walked to a nearby Porta Potty. Other-Abner said something into the lock, opened the door, and closed it behind him. I got close enough to hear what turned out to be Other-Amanda walking up to the same door and leaning into the lock to whisper something.

"Mavis Beacon teaches typing."

Then, an electronic voice quietly responded through the lock. "Voice analysis confirmed. Entrance granted, Agent JOHNNY."

Whoa.

I did what I *thought* was the smart move and walked up to the same Porta Potty. Leaning into the lock, I said, "Mavis Beacon teaches typing."

The robot voice seemed to take three eternities to respond but finally said that voice analysis was confirmed. "Entrance granted, Agent SWIM."

"Dumb name," I mumbled to myself.

Taking one step, I fell into the hole that had opened up in front of the toilet.

I slid down for about thirty feet before falling out of a tube ungracefully, only getting to my feet in time to realize I was in a cold, humid cavern and had interrupted a debriefing of some sort.

Agents JOHNNY and SWIM stood before a futuristic projection that showed a backlit shadow speaking in a disguised voice and giving instructions of some kind.

"We're *spies!?!?*" I couldn't help saying out loud. *Is that pride I'm feeling?*

"I told you he'd figure it out," my doppelgänger said.

I was beginning to think I didn't like this Other-Abner. As I looked over to Other-Amanda for some help, she and Other-Abner both drew their weapons.

They fired.

I woke up in bed in a cold sweat, panting.

Wow. What a dream.

I had to write it down. I stirred my Amanda from her sleep next to me.

"Babe, why are you waking me up?!" she asked.

"I think I've got a cool band name!"

"Go to sleeeeeeep!"

Amanda

YEARS AGO, BACK WHEN ABNER and I lived tiny paycheck to tiny paycheck, back when playing shows felt like a test of the worthiness of our dreams, before we had a team or a plan, before this book was ever even on the wish list, my parents drove us to a little show in Fairfield, Connecticut. This made me nervous.

It was one of those shows where a friend had pulled a favor for another friend and got us a few minutes opening for another friend. It wasn't glamorous by any means, but we were thrilled for the chance, because at this point, all we had were chances. No one there would have heard us before, which meant, of course, that probably no one would care. It's what we had signed up for. What we hadn't signed up for was having my parents sitting front row center. I loved them but had begged them to stay home. Because if things went south, I wanted to be able to forget it. I didn't want sympathy pats after the show. I wanted to blend in at a local pub with a beer and a small, unassuming shot of self-pity.

I did my best to persuade them into changing their minds. The more I tried, the more they insisted on coming. My dad rented an SUV, and Abner and I crammed in the back with his guitar and our show clothes, like little babies heading to their first day of school, excited but preemptively ashamed.

As we got closer, my nervousness grew exponentially. Would my parents see me as a failure if no one liked our set? If we sounded horrible, would they feel bad for me, or worse, would they feel bad for themselves, like they had failed somehow in their musical parenting? What if the monitors were bad and we couldn't hear? What if we knew we were sucking only because we could see the panic in my parents' faces? There just didn't seem to be a lot of good options there. And a lot of ways things could go wrong.

I let the current of doubt and fear pull me along silently as we merged onto the Merritt Parkway, getting closer and closer to the venue. Looking straight ahead down the road, my mom finally broke the silence.

Abner

AMANDA'S MOM ALWAYS HAD A way with words. She was a writer, after all. My mother-in-law spoke casual poetry when she encouraged us. "These are the good old days! You'll never get these days back," she said. "One day you'll be on a bus, playing shows every night, and nights like this one will be a far-off memory, a sweet memory. I'd rather be here for these small shows than the big ones that are sure to come. You don't get to come back to your first shows ever again. These are the good old days."

There was a sense of gratitude that stuck to our ribs when she said it. "Despise not the days of small beginnings," the Good Book says. Boy, was she right.

I think that today we're still just getting started in our career, with many triumphs and letdowns ahead of us. But one thing we'll never get back is *right now.*

I was telling someone yesterday how we're moving my mom and sister out here to Los Angeles so we can spend more time together. He encouraged me to enjoy this opportunity. *"Lo que está en el pasado ya no existe,"* he said ("What is in the past no longer exists"). More practically it meant, "You can't change the stuff that's behind you."

These are the good old days.

It's hard sometimes to take a deep breath and allow ourselves to be immersed fully in how great the great things are. There's always the temptation to add, "Sure, *but . . .*" to the tail of any positive thought. When Donna said, "These are the good old days," she was forcing us to stop the "Sure, but . . ." part of the phrase. *This* is great. This moment. We'll never have this again. It's become a creed and a reminder that no matter what lies ahead, we have something to be grateful for. Something to cherish right in front of us.

It's the secret to making home anywhere you find yourself—even on a tour bus going sixty-five miles an hour down a stretch of highway that has no humanity within one hundred miles in either direction. When we appreciate how precious right now is, we begin to get a glimpse of just how sacred right now is: raising our babies and chasing dreams, hopefully teaching them all the while that they can live their lives with full hearts, no matter how small this moment seems in the shadow of dreams yet to be lived.

Fulfillment doesn't come with the things you can hang on a wall. It comes with the fullness of living that is attained only with true gratitude and contentment.

These are truly the good old days.

Make no mistake
We'll live while we're young
We'll chase down the sun
Hands off the brake
Oh, we can die when we're done
Let's live while we're young
Let's live while we're young.

THESE ARE TRULY THE GOOD OL' DAYS

ACKNOWLEDGMENTS

IF YOU'VE READ ALL THE WORDS in this book, you may have noticed a theme. JOHNNYSWIM is a community endeavor. As much as we two have dreamed, worked, and chased our passions, those pursuits would have been cute but futile without our team and family. Without the slingshot force of our champions, we would have crawled and dawdled along our path.

We've put off writing these acknowledgments until the very end because the task seemed so daunting. We are like the frame of a car. Naming and thanking each component that makes us run with such luxury seems impossible, so we're narrowing it down. Chances are, some of you reading this deserve a mention here. Please know that you were probably thanked in our hearts, but yeah, sorry, maybe next book you'll be thanked in words.

Okay, here we go. This book would be nothing without our kids. Our life without you, Joaquin, Luna, and Paloma, would probably not be as fun to read about. You have brought the adventure, inspiration, and cuteness that really makes folks happy. You certainly make us happy. You also force us to wake up early, which has given us more time in the day to get stuff done, like writing this book. I hope it sells a million, bajillion copies so you three perfect babies can have in- finite Lego, epic vacations together, and the best trust fund of all time.

Our managers, Jay King and John Meneilly, are dope. But you guys already know how much we love you, because we gave you a whole chapter. I hope this book sells a million, bajillion copies so we can all have houses next to each other in Park City.

Our community of family and friends at home and our tour family on the road keep us sane, protected, grounded, and loved. You guys are really the heart and soul of how and why we do what we do. The joy and connection we have in being loved by all of you is the same joy and connection we hope to share when we write and play music. We hope this book sells a million, bajillion copies so we can all just take private jets to every show.

Specifically, thanks to Mike McGlaflin and Darren Lau, our brother-in-law and our best friend, respectively. We are grateful to you both for being cooler and much more tech savvy than we'll ever be. We hope this book sells a million, bajillion copies so Mike can finally live on the West Side.

Home Sweet Road would not be anywhere in the realm of reality if not for you, Travis Thrasher. Who knew, all the way back in 2014 when you watched us play in the rain at Lollapalooza, that you

would be having to find ways every other day to gently put fires under our butts to write, that you would be finding the valuable turds among all our ramblings and encouraging us to polish them into something we could share and that would hopefully inspire others, and that you would become a friend and homey. I hope this book sells a million, bajillion copies so we can write and produce our own Season 4 of *Dark*.

And last but not least, thanks to our team at Convergent/Penguin Random House for believing in us, putting up with our interpretation of deadlines, and making this process fun. We hope we sell a million, bajillion copies so we can do this all over again.

Unless otherwise noted, photos are courtesy of the authors' personal collection.

pages vii, 7, 9 (top), 123 (bottom), 127 (top left; bottom right), 131 (bottom), 132 (top), 139 (bottom), 140 (bottom), 153 (top right; bottom right), 214, 218, 219, 237 (bottom): photos by Amy Waters; page x: photo by Nolan Feldpausch; pages xi, 78, 128 (bottom), 171 (bottom), 214 (top right): photos by Rachel Jonas; pages xii, xiii, 2, 3, 12, 13, 16, 17, 36, 37, 66, 67, 72, 81, 87, 124–125, 127 (top right), 128 (top), 132 (bottom left), 153 (left), 166 (top), 212, 220, 222, 224, 225, 226, 227, 228, 229, 234, 235: photos copyright © Darren Lau, Photographer to the Stars; pages 10, 14, 19, 39, 244: photos by Camille Blinn; pages 22, 23, 32, 92, 115, 116, 118, 119: photos by Tec Petaja Photography; pages 35, 82, 197: photos by Bruce Sudano; pages 43, 168, 200, 201, 203, 206, 207: photos by G L Askew II; pages 52, 53: photos by Concepción Studios; pages 84, 86, 136 (top left): photos by Tim Cho; pages 136 (bottom left), 166 (bottom): photos by Noah Torralba; page 151 (bottom left): photo by Maria Berlin; pages 70, 165, 189: photos by Jay King; pages 176–177: photos by Rachel Heisel; pages 209–210: photos by Tessa Reyes Benz; page 223: photo by Madi Rae Jones; page 232: photos by Brad Moore /BMOORE VISUALS; pages 249, 250, 251: photos by Brandon Smith Media

JOHNNYSWIM COMPRISES HUS-band and wife ABNER RAMIREZ and AMANDA SUDANO RAMIREZ. The pair met in Nashville in 2005, and soon their music began appearing on TV shows ranging from *Hawaii Five-O* to *Fixer Upper* with Chip and Joanna Gaines. Along the way, they garnered acclaim from *Rolling Stone,* NPR, *The New York Times, HuffPost, Nylon, DuJour,* and VH1, in addition to performing on NBC's *The Tonight Show with Jay Leno, Today, Conan,* and more. With their full-length album debut, *Diamonds,* came the hit song "Home," which became the *Fixer Upper* theme song, and "Diamonds," which has been featured on *America's Got Talent.* JOHNNYSWIM possesses the "sparkle of natural-born stage performers" (NPR) and has cultivated a devoted audience who pack the duo's sold-out shows.

JOHNNYSWIM.COM

ABOUT THE AUTHORS